Principles of Preaching is one of t[...] I have seen on the subject. Written by an experienced pastor/preacher, this work throbs with the author's heartbeat for training pastors, especially bi-vocational pastors, how to be more effective preachers. Regardless of age or experience, all who preach the Word will find help here. I hope this work finds its way to the shelf of every pastor.

DAVID L. ALLEN, Dean
School of Theology
Southwestern Baptist Theological Seminary, Fort Worth, Texas

Principles of Preaching is a totally unique perspective on the sacred art of proclamation. Mike Boyd writes out of a rich background of a consideration of these issues from the viewpoint of years of pastoral preaching. Christ is thematic for Pastor Boyd who in this monograph makes all of his own manifold talents support the preaching assignment. Here is a book that will assist the pastor.

PAIGE PATTERSON, President
Southwestern Baptist Theological Seminary, Fort Worth, Texas

"Preaching is not the making of a sermon and delivering that, but the making of a preacher and delivering that!" so said Bishop William Quayle. Mike Boyd has made a good case for developing both preacher and sermon in his book *Principles of Preaching.* As a professor of preaching, I look for books that have a balance between admonishments for being good ministers of Jesus Christ and practical advice for developing good sermons about Jesus Christ. Dr. Boyd's book does just that. Using the same homiletical skills that he teaches, Dr. Boyd offers important principles every preacher should apply to be a faithful herald of God. He also outlines and explains simple but effective methods of developing expository sermons that explain the biblical text and apply to the lives of real people in the pew. I look forward to sharing this work with my students and using in my pulpit ministry.

JERE PHILLIPS, Professor of Theology/Director of Extensions
Mid-America Baptist Theological Seminary, Cordova, Tennessee

PRINCIPLES
of Preaching

(handwritten inscription)

To Jimmy

Blessings
Mildo Boyd

1 Cor 1:2 3

A GUIDEBOOK *for* COMMUNICATING BIBLICAL TRUTH

PRINCIPLES
of Preaching

MIKE BOYD

CROSSBOOKS

CrossBooks™
A Division of LifeWay
1663 Liberty Drive
Bloomington, IN 47403
www.crossbooks.com
Phone: 1-866-879-0502

First published by CrossBooks 05/29/2013

ISBN: 978-1-4627-2560-1 (sc)
ISBN: 978-1-4627-2562-5 (hc)
ISBN: 978-1-4627-2561-8 (e)

Library of Congress Control Number: 2013903762

Printed in the United States of America

This book is printed on acid-free paper.

Certain stock imagery © Thinkstock.
Any people depicted in stock imagery provided by Thinkstock are models,
and such images are being used for illustrative purposes only.

Unless otherwise stated, all Scripture citations are taken
from the Holman Christian Standard Bible.

Scripture citations marked KJV are from the King James Version.

Scripture citations marked NIV are from the New International Version.

TABLE OF CONTENTS

To my devoted wife, Sandy Boyd, who has faithfully
ministered by my side for over 35 years,

To my grandmother, Ethyl Lowrie Gamble,
who assisted financially in my theological education,

To my sons, Trey and Matt Boyd, who survived unique challenges
of growing up in a pastor's home and who are my heroes,

To my daughter-in-law, Kristin Boyd, and my wife's parents,
Aaron and Melba Long, whom I love and appreciate,

To my deceased father, Miles Boyd, Sr., and my mother,
Ruth Boyd, who raised me in a Christian home,

To my administrative assistant, Jane McPherson,
who spent countless hours on the details of this project, and

To my church family, Wallace Memorial Baptist Church
in Knoxville, Tennessee, who offers me the privilege of preaching.

Principles of Preaching is designed to move
the truths of God's Word from the
Heart of Heaven to the hearts of humans.

FOREWORD

In 2008 and 2009 the groundwork was done for the creation of the J. Harold Smith Pastor Training Center. It had long been the God-inspired dream to establish a training program for bi-vocational pastors who could not afford either the time or money to pursue a full-time seminary education. The Radio Bible Hour, established as a Baptist Radio Ministry in 1935 by J. Harold Smith, provided the funds to start the Center, and helped in the development of its curriculum. Men such as Dr. Walter Crouch of Carson-Newman College, Dr. Dean Haun of First Baptist Church, Morristown, TN, and the author of this text, Dr. Mike Boyd, shared the vision and the desire to work toward the creation and development of the Smith Center. They agreed to help teach, organize, publicize, and support with their Godly counsel, the creation and development of the Smith Center for Pastor Training.

More than 70% of the pastors in Tennessee are working a secular job, in addition to the responsibilities of pastoring a church, and most have families. Their financial resources are often limited. Almost all of them have a burning desire to be better pastors, to know more about God's Word, and to have mentoring and counsel from more experienced pastors. The Smith Center is working to address these needs in several ways.

The course fees are kept relatively low. The classes are held in convenient locations, on evenings or Saturdays. The teachers are experienced in the pastorate, and in the skills of pastoring. The use of video and audio recordings allows the student maximum flexibility to catch up when the pastoral responsibilities cause them to miss a scheduled class. More important is the philosophy of the Smith Center that honors the calling of the pastors, and that upholds and honors the Bible as God's Word.

Principles of Preaching reflects the Smith Center philosophy. It is concise but packed with practical and relevant information. It will prove valuable to those who are considering a call to ministry, as well as those who are already laboring in the pastorate. The text will strengthen preaching and pastoral practice, but it will also encourage a deeper relationship with Jesus Christ as one reads it.

Our desire in the Smith Center is that each class meeting, as well as each learning assignment, would draw both the teacher and students closer to the Lord. Only in Him will our learning experience be inspired and blessed. *Principles of Preaching* can serve this kind of learning environment. The book was a blessing to me as I read it, and I know it will enrich the lives of those who use it to make them stronger servants of Jesus Christ. Thank you, Dr. Boyd, for developing and writing this material, and for your love of the Lord and the lost which inspires your ministry.

J. DONALD SMITH, President
Radio Bible Hour, Inc., Newport, Tennessee

INTRODUCTION

The preparation of teaching a class, *Principles of Preaching*, to bi-vocational pastors has caused me to pause and take a deep introspective look at what I have been doing for the past 35 years. This is not the course I chose for myself. The lifelong dream of becoming an international businessman would become lost in fulfilling what has become a very complex and demanding vocation. While verbally reflecting on some difficult ministry matters, a well-meaning parishioner commented, "You chose what you do for a living." The statement has never been lost in the files of my mind. Indeed, I did NOT choose what I do. I responded in obedience, but I did not choose it. God designed it. God chose me. I simply responded, "YES!"

Interestingly, I have never lost that passion for global impact. The business portion of my D.N.A. has not been wasted either. While performing what God has called me to do, I have been privileged to personally visit over 20 foreign countries. There have been countless people impacted through various mission/ministry organizations and activities. A good number of former staff and "preacher boys" are actively involved in pastorates and leading ministries that affect thousands every week. I would have never dreamed that God could take a simple person such as myself and allow such impact. To God be the glory!

Now, I have the opportunity to assist some of God's chosen men who have been called to do the same. I do not approach this task with an unrealistic feeling that I have all of the answers. Indeed, I do not. However, I do know some of the questions that must be addressed. This material is not designed to impress scholars or depress those who may not be fortunate enough to have formal education. It is simply an attempt to solidify and enhance those to whom have been given the highest calling in the world: "to communicate the truths of the Bible to human beings in need of a word from God." To HIM be all glory!

MIKE BOYD
Knoxville, Tennessee

CHAPTER 1

CALLING

The Doctrine of Vocation

J esus said to them all, "If anyone wants to come with Me, he must deny himself, take up his cross daily, and follow Me" (Luke 9:23).

Vocation – Merriam-Webster Online Dictionary offers a secular understanding of "vocation." It has the following properties:
- Originates from the Latin "vocation" meaning "to summons"
- *Vocare* means "to call"
- *Vox* means "voice"

Calling – Definitions of "calling" include:
- A summons or strong inclination to a particular state or course of action
- Especially a divine call to the religious life
- An entry into the priesthood or a religious order
- The work in which a person is regularly employed
- Occupation: a special function

One cannot overlook the strong religious overtones of the word. Historically, one's vocation is tied to the calling God places on one's life.

Calling to Salvation

The *calling to salvation* is an important place to begin. The *calling* may be the only thing that keeps us going. A pastor can always return to the basic bedrock of God's anointment and appointment in His service. All salvation begins with *conviction*. Individuals cannot be saved until they are aware of their lostness, *but* this is not the job of the preacher. This is the job of the Holy Spirit!

Conviction is the job of the Holy Spirit!

Conviction - *the awareness of being what the Bible terms as "lost"*
In John 16:8, Jesus says, "When He comes, *He will convict* the world about sin..." (emphasis added). Without this conviction, nothing else *spiritually* can happen. It is not the preacher's job or the spouse's job to convict someone. The Holy Spirit's movement in and around a person brings to light the reality of sin. Sin is an inside job. It is a matter of the heart. The Holy Spirit works internally to bring a person to understand *lostness* as it relates to being alienated from God.

God uses proclamation of the Word of God to bring conviction. When the Holy Spirit worked at Pentecost, He empowered Peter to present a tremendous mosaic of God's design for humans. Acts 2:37 says, "When they heard this, they were pierced to the heart and said...'Brothers, what must we do?'" Conviction is always a prelude to conversion.

Communication - *simply being convicted is not enough*

Someone somewhere must communicate the gospel message. Romans 10:14 says, "But how can they call on Him in whom they have not believed? And how can they believe without hearing about Him?"

1 Corinthians 1:21 says, "For since, in God's wisdom, the world did not know God through wisdom, God was pleased to save those who believe through the foolishness of the message preached."

The bottom line is that in order for someone to have salvation, there must be a conviction of sin and a communication that God's Son (Jesus) paid the price for that sin on a cross. That's why the Bible says, "Go, therefore, and make disciples of all nations" (Matthew 28:19) which might be paraphrased, "Tell 'em!"

Commitment/Conversion - *John 3:16 - pisteuo - believe...trust in action*

Simply offering intellectual consent to the message regarding Jesus' advent, death, burial, and resurrection is not enough. The Bible confirms, "The demons also believe–and they shudder" (James 2:19).

Someone has suggested that the distance between heaven and hell is only eighteen inches—the distance between the head and the heart.

A conversion experience requires a commitment that involves the entire life. "Then Jesus said to them all, 'If anyone wants to come with Me, he must deny himself, take up his cross daily, and follow Me'" (Luke 9:23). Jesus is saying that one must commit his entire life to Him. Luke 9:23 is a verse of...

o   deliverance
o   discipleship
o   dedication

We are *not* saved to laziness!

Consecration - *saved to serve*

A person is not only saved in order to go to heaven but also saved in order to be set apart for service. We are not made "holy" just so we can talk about our holiness. We are saved to serve! Once we have been born again and have been especially gifted *spiritually*, there is something for us to do.

Someone asked, "When we get saved, is that the end of it?" Yes, the *front end*, that is! When we follow the Lord in believer's baptism, we then set out on a journey of growth and service. These two go hand in hand. Philippians 2:12b-13 states, "...work out your own salvation with fear and trembling. For it is God who is working in you, [enabling you] both to will and to act for His good purpose."

We do not need to be afraid of this verse. The Apostle Paul is *not* saying that we work *for* our salvation. He is saying that we work *from* our salvation.

Calling to Service

Identifying the Call - *spiritually gifted*

At conversion, every believer is given a dominant *spiritual* gift. Proclamation of the gospel is the responsibility of every believer. However, God calls different people to differing vocations. The call to preach is one that cannot be manufactured. It is a result of being *spiritually* gifted. This gift did not exist prior to conversion. Gifts are not to be confused with talents. Some of the finest expositors of scripture have not necessarily been the most talented of communicators. However, as led by the Spirit, they become a powerhouse for God.

How do we know if we have been called to preach? There are some points of *spiritual* engagement that verify and validate our calling:

- o **The Bible:** The first point of *spiritual* engagement is the Bible. As a child of God reads the Bible, there arises a compulsion to preach. The prophet Jeremiah says, "His message becomes a fire burning in my heart, shut up in my bones. I become tired of holding it in, and I cannot prevail" (Jeremiah 20:9).

o **The Prayer Closet:** The second place of affirmation in the call to preach is the prayer closet. Agonizing in prayer over this calling is difficult but necessary. Not to take time to pray about the matter will certainly short circuit the process. It is in the quietness of our time with God that He affirms what we are to do. Jesus would often go to predetermined places in order to be alone with His Heavenly Father.

o **The Local Church:** The third location that affirms the call to preach is the local church. Men in the New Testament were set apart to carry on the official work of the church. Demonstration of God's call to preach will be evident in the lives of those with whom an individual has worked and served over a number of years. Denominations and associations are not in the business of ordination. Local churches are where the rubber meets the road. If there is not positive reinforcement in one's "home church," then there should be some concern regarding the calling.

o **The Listeners:** A fourth confirmation comes from those who have heard an individual expound. While trial sermons are questionable practices, they do offer insight if seasoned "hearers" place a confirmation on an individual's ability to "rightly divide the word of truth" (2 Timothy 2:15). If nobody is listening, that may be a sign that something has gone askew.

Although these four areas—the Bible, the prayer closet, the local church, and the listeners—are not exclusive, they do offer a good barometer of where an individual's calling might lie in regards to the preaching ministry. Certainly there could be exceptions; however, they are most likely rare and isolated. Always assume that someone is listening.

Jack Taylor, a Deeper Life movement proponent of the 1970s and 80s told me, "If you can do anything else, do it." But somewhere in the bowels of our spirit, there is a compulsion that will not allow us to do anything else. The disciples were ordered not to continue preaching "in the name of Jesus" (Acts 4:18). Their response: "We are unable to stop speaking about what we have seen and heard" (Acts 4:20). Now that sounds like a divine calling to me!

Implementing the Call - *a call to preach is a call to prepare*

One of the great frustrations expressed by those entering the ministry as well as those who prepare multiple messages each week are the questions: *Where do I begin? How do I know what to preach and when to preach it?* Such issues will be addressed in subsequent sessions; however, there are some basics that apply regardless of where one's ministry responsibility lies on the continuum.

A call to preach is a call to prepare. Effective biblical communication means effective biblical preparation. Several issues related to implementation will be mentioned and explored further in later sessions. However, as we begin to think about responding to God's call, an understanding of the following concepts will be most helpful.

Personal Devotional Life

In order to speak for God, one needs to walk with God. This involves prayer, meditation, and Bible study. Effective ministry cannot begin with the life experiences or sermons of other people. It must begin with one's own genuine communion with God.

A preacher should speak from the overflow of his own walk with God. If material is used that comes from outside sources (someone else's sermon), remember to:

- o Admit it.
- o Do it seldom.
- o If possible, gain permission from the original source or preacher.

Psalm 1:1-3 offers a biblical foundation upon which any preacher may build. Its principles are sound, succinct, and speak for themselves. We would all do well to take some time and pour over this text:

> "How happy is the man
> who does not follow the advice of the wicked,
> or take the path of sinners,
> or join a group of mockers!"

Pay close attention. Here is the key to building a biblical foundation:

> *"Instead, his delight is in the LORD's instruction,*
> *and he meditates on it day and night.*

> He is like a tree planted beside streams of water
> that bears its fruit in season
> and whose leaf does not wither.
> Whatever he does prospers."

Perhaps we should ask:

- o What principles are being taught in this text?
- o What is the writer experiencing that relates to me?
- o How can I apply this text as a beginning point for my messages?

o   What is the result of activating the principles taught in
this text?

Pastors need to be preaching out of the overflow of their own
personal relationship with God. This can only happen when adequate
devotional time is spent with Him.

Expect interferences and interruptions!

*The Importance of Study: How can we preach unless we are willing to
prepare?*
The amount of time needed to prepare a message fluctuates. There
are always interferences and interruptions. However, who would want
to fly on an airplane designed and built by competent people who
were not giving their best? In turn, who wants to listen to a speaker
talk about a vital and important subject who has not taken the time
to learn all he can about a particular text? There is no substitute for
prolonged and accurate investigation of the Word of God:

> "Be diligent to present yourself approved to God,
> a worker who doesn't need to be ashamed,
> correctly teaching the word of truth" (2 Timothy 2:15).

A young college ministerial student reportedly drove from Union
University in Jackson, Tennessee to meet with the famous legend, Dr.
R.G. Lee, late pastor of Bellevue Baptist Church in Memphis. During
conversation, the student remarked that Dr. Lee was a very gifted
communicator of God's Word. Dr. Lee scoffed and took the student
to the pastor's study. There were legal pads of notes and books all over

the place. Dr. Lee remarked, "Son, does this look like a gift, or does it look like hard work?"

Dr. Lee was one of the most noted biblical orators of the 20th Century; however, his point was that it takes toil and labor in preparation. Even the Bible says, "A *worker* (emphasis added) who doesn't need to be ashamed."

Finding A Place

Jesus had places He would frequent in order to be alone with His Heavenly Father. Luke 11:1 says, "He was praying in *a certain place* (emphasis added)." The text indicates that this was no ordinary place. It was somewhere Jesus would go purposefully to get away and commune with the Father. The mountains of Galilee and the Mount of Olives provided such places for Jesus.

Every preacher needs a place where He can go and meet God. It needs to be a place that is easily accessible and private. In today's world, there probably needs to be not only books, but electronics for meditative music, internet, biblical study aids, and adequate materials to thoroughly investigate the text.

One more thought needs to be considered about the word "place" in Luke 11:1. While I believe it was a physical place, there may also need to be a certain place in time on our calendars *when* we schedule to meet God. Experience teaches that Satan will bring many good things our way to keep us from the best thing. There needs to be a physical and chronological place where (and when) we are unimpeded and can do the work God has called us to do.

Issues Facing Listeners

The story is told of three people who went to a particular church looking for life answers. One was an alcoholic needing a word on how to defeat its evils. A second was a young girl considering yielding her body to further her career. The third was a young man who had lost everything and was now contemplating suicide. All in the same worship service (unknowingly to each other or the preacher), they heard a message entitled "Who Wrote the Book of Hebrews?" Each individual left without any answers for hope and fell prey to their personal issues.

The point of this story is that the preacher must be sensitive to life's issues within the community in which he serves. A pastor cannot possibly know all of the pitfalls which plague church members, but there should be sensitivity to what the needs are in particular congregations. This cannot possibly happen unless there is contact and interaction with the community and with people.

> **Delight in the LORD's instruction**
> **...meditate on it day and night!**

CHAPTER 2

COMMANDMENT

The Biblical Philosophy of Ministry

H e said to him, "*Love the Lord your God with all your heart, with all your soul, and with all your mind.* This is the greatest and most important commandment" (Matthew 22:37-38).

The Greatest Commandment

These two verses encapsulate the basic biblical philosophy that underlies one's ministry when truly following the Holy Spirit. Addressing the student body at Southwestern Baptist Theological Seminary (Fall 2009), I communicated my heart's desire was to bring the very same message Jesus would bring if He were standing there bodily. This text was used because it is the answer to a most foundational question: "Which commandment in the law is the *greatest?*" (Matthew 22:36).

The significance of that question lies in the meaning of the word "greatest." The Greek (*megas*) offers the meanings of large, mighty, strong, or significant. The religious leaders were asking Jesus about the most significant mandate from God. It stands to reason that this was top on the list of what was on God's mind and heart.

Ministry (preaching) must be a derivative of what is on God's heart. Preaching should neither flow from personal preference nor an audience's agenda. It most certainly should begin in the throne room of the universe. It must begin in the very heart and mind of God. In order to preach strong and effective biblical messages, we must have a strong and biblical philosophy. That philosophy is established as we seek God's mind and heart.

Key to biblical preaching is LISTENING!

The Shema - a declaration of faith in One God
The answer is not found in the most famous list of laws known to mankind. Rather it is a quote from *The Shema*. *The Shema* is a transliteration of the Hebrew word, "to hear." *The Shema* is found in Deuteronomy 6:4-9:

> "*Listen*...The LORD our God, the LORD is One. Love the LORD your God with all your heart, with all your soul, and with all your strength. These words that I am giving you today are to be in your heart. Repeat them to your children. Talk about them when you sit in your house and when you walk along the road, when you lie down and when you get up. Bind them as a sign on your hand and let them be a symbol on your forehead. Write them on the doorposts of your house and on your gates."

While Jesus may not have answered this question as the people expected, He communicated a truth denoting God's priority. Several things stand out with His answer:

- ○ *Jesus did not* allow the crowd to dictate His message.
- ○ *Jesus did* address their question. God's voice should always be ready to offer biblical solutions to life's questions. 1 Peter 3:15 says, "Be ready always to give an answer to every man that asketh you a reason of the hope that is in you…" (KJV).
- ○ *Jesus relied upon scripture* to be foundational in His answer. Jesus modeled a communication technique of scriptural referencing. When portions of scripture are quoted by Jesus, one needs to look at the meaning of the entire text.

The Shema is the basic and essential creed of Judaism. Every Jewish service opened with it. As Jewish children committed verses to memory, this would be the first. Personal and liturgical life would be built on the truths described within.

Some say we are not a creedal people—Hogwash! "Creed" is a set of fundamental beliefs, e.g., Martin Luther's *The Ninety-Five Theses* written in 1517.

If the Bible doesn't say it, neither should we!

A young preacher asked a mature deacon to critique a message. The elderly deacon kindly responded, "Your comments were correct, but much too often you used the words 'I think.' It would be much better to use the words 'The Bible says' and if the Bible doesn't say it, you should not either."

Alternate philosophies would include: anger, social concerns, and political views. Today's politicians have taken *spiritual* issues and made them political. Then the same politicians tell us that we cannot 'speak out' because of separation of God and Government! WRONG!

Love God ~ Love People

This foundational philosophy commandment ought also to be the structure upon which every sermon is built. Each biblical message should be crafted in a manner where it is sifted through the truth of loving God and loving people. Jesus insists that in the mind of God, this is the most important element. As I prepare, the question must be asked, "Am I developing something that is consistent with loving God and loving people? It is not an "either-or." Both elements must be present.

If this is so vital, an in depth understanding of this text becomes necessary. Let's read it again and then unpack it:

> "Jesus said, 'Love the Lord your God with all your heart, with all your soul, and with all your mind. This is the greatest and most important commandment. The second is like it: **Love your neighbor as yourself'**" (Matthew 22:37-39).

Is the message consistent?
Love God and Love People!

The Second Is Like It

Jesus' answer yields two truths that are inseparable. Jesus combines the two by saying, "The second is *like* it." The word "like" (*homoios*) is derived from a root word meaning "together" which signifies that what is about to be said corresponds to what has just been said.

To separate loving God and loving people is to negate both. To claim a love for God without a love for people will simply produce a communication disconnection. In reality, the deeper our love is for God, the more substantive is our love for people.

> "And we have this command from Him: the one who loves God must also love his brother" (1 John 4:21).

On the other hand, to love people and only offer lip service for love of God is shallow at best and virtually theologically impossible. Why? "...because God is love" (1 John 4:8). Consequently, love for God is incomplete without a genuine love for people. Therefore, we must examine both.

Love the Lord Your God

Make no mistake, our love for God is a direct response of His love for us. 1 John 4:19 says, "We love because He first loved us." There are three practical components to loving God:
1. Love God through His Word.
2. Love God through His Will.
3. Love God His Way.

> Love God by loving His Word!

God's Word - *delight in His gift*

The first practical component to love God is found in loving His Word. The Psalmist said, "His delight is in the LORD's instruction, and he *meditates*[1] on it day and night" (Psalm 1:2). No doubt, the Word of God becomes an object of passion for those who love God.

While my wife and I were dating, we were separated for a year prior to our wedding day. She wrote me beautiful letters. (This was prior to the Facebook, texting, Twitter, and email era.) As each letter arrived, I carefully read and re-read it. I examined every word and phrase. I could even hear her tender voice speaking what she had written on the page. Why? I loved her!

God has written us a love letter. Because of our love for Him, we must spend time exploring and meditating in His Word. As we mature in our relationship, we can hear His voice loudly (although not audibly) speaking to us.

Preaching is not a selective activity. We are not free to simply engage in dialogue of opinions, preferences, or book reviews. While listening to messages of other preachers can be helpful, it may also become harmful. If one is simply going to rehash something that someone else has done, why not just show the video? It will be better done than you or I could do it! Why? This is what God has given to someone else in His love relationship with an individual.

Love God by loving His Word. *There is NO short cut to genuine biblical preaching!* It takes time and diligence in the Word of God.

God's Will - *delight in doing His Will*

The second practical component is to love God's Will. Jesus said, "If you love Me, you will *keep*[2] My commandments" (John 14:15). When we love someone, we strive to grant his (or her) heart's desire.

---

1   "Meditates" (*hagah*): Keeps on going on. Qal: Simple statement. Mood: Imperfect.

2   "Keep" (*tereo*): To attend, to carefully guard, to observe. Aorist: point in time. Active; participation. Imperative; a command; e.g., "I'm not asking; I'm telling." Know it! Do it!

What is your attitude towards God's will?

Nothing can quench God's Spirit in a message any quicker than an attitude towards God about where He places His servants. If one studies the original preachers, none was in the easiest of circumstances.

- o Remember Jonah not wanting to preach to the people of Nineveh...*What do you suppose was Jonah's attitude?*
- o *What about Stephen?* The Bible tells us that Stephen was content as the last stone lacerated his skull: "...he fell asleep" (Acts 7:60).

In current contemporary culture, many preachers are working harder to move than they are to allow God's will to be done in them right where they are. Difficult as it may be, we must learn to bloom where we are planted.

That was the motif of the Apostle Paul. He declared, "...I have learned to be content in whatever circumstances I am" (Philippians 4:11). Paul practiced what he preached. In Acts 16:25, Paul and Silas were in a dungeon cell. *What were they doing?* "...praying and singing hymns to God." *Then what happened?* People were saved!

> Preaching is more powerful
> when it is done with confidence,
> compassion, and contentment rather
> than with critical resentment!

God's Way - *delight as He works in and through you*

The third practical component of loving God is to have affection for God's Way. Often we desire to manufacture results. He says, "...

your ways are not My ways" (Isaiah 55:8). Ultimately, we must trust God to do as He desires in the manner He desires. *Spirituality* cannot be defined with human orchestration or programming. *Spirituality* is a process. As our love for God grows, so does our love for the way He works in and through us. The Psalmist offers a mature analysis when he says, "I *delight*[3] to do Your will, my God; Your instruction resides within me" (Psalm 40:8).

Even when we do not understand, we need to keep on going with God. It is not necessary for us to comprehend what is happening. When we love God, we must simply trust Him to do what only He can do.

How is it that these three practical expressions become a reality in our lives? Jesus articulates them successfully:

- o   We are to love God with all our heart — *Passion!*
- o   We are to love God with all our soul — *Person!*
- o   We are to love God with all our mind — *Perspective!*

A painted fire never warmed anyone!

Loving Him with all our passion

First, passion for God is no option for a called preacher of the gospel. To love God with all our "heart" yields a tremendous passion for Him. We cannot wait to be with Him, speak with Him, and advocate for Him. Every second of the day, God is on our mind.

The prophet Jeremiah delivers perhaps the clearest and most compelling case of having passion for God. He says, "His message becomes a fire burning in my heart, shut up in my bones. I become tired of holding it in, and I cannot prevail" (Jeremiah 20:9). The

---

3   "Delight" (*chaphets*): Take pleasure in, desire to be with. Qal: Simple statement. Mood: Perfect. Complete, absolute, fulfilling.

Psalmist adds to this imagery with the concept of thirst: "As a deer longs for streams of water, so I *long*⁴ for You, God" (Psalm 42:1).

We cannot manufacture a passion for God. When we believe in something so deeply that we pant for it, our passion becomes contagious. Richard Jackson, a famous artist acknowledged, "A painted fire never warmed anyone." Passion develops as our personal relationship with Him strengthens. If we are not truly hungry for God, we will communicate that void to our listeners. *If, we, the messengers are not fully committed, who will truly believe our spoken words?*

Loving Him with all our person

Secondly, our entire person must be committed to the Lord. We do not have a soul; we are a soul. "Then the LORD God formed the man out of the dust from the ground and breathed the breath of life into his nostrils, and the man became a living being" (Genesis 2:7). We are living beings who happen to have physical bodies.

Loving God with all our soul means that we are willing to be deprived of comforts for the cause of Christ and take up His cross daily (Luke 9:23). Preaching the gospel cannot be driven by convenience. Neither should there be guilt when conveniences might arise, but that cannot be the motivation for ministry.

Every fiber of who we are must be committed to God's calling on our life. Jesus said, "No one who puts his hand to the plow and looks back is fit for the kingdom of God" (Luke 9:62).

Loving Him with all our perspective

Thirdly, we must develop a perspective that mirrors with God's perspective. Loving God with "all my mind" means that I serve due diligence in the pastor's study. The intellectual development of going deeper in God's Word allows me to gain the mind of Christ. 1 Corinthians 2:16 says, "We have the mind of Christ." The word

---

4   "Long" (*arag*): Long for, pant; relentless and run after something; to yearn.

"mind" (*nous*) means understanding. The same root word is used by Jesus in Matthew. It has the prefix "*dia*" added which means "thorough." The idea is to encompass and investigate with a thorough process. The result is that one gains a perspective that agrees with God's.

Pastoring

Pastoring near a nuclear defense facility affords me opportunity to serve many Christian employees and engineers. One man indicated that he worked for an entire day on a math problem which would help to secure our nation and eliminate disaster.

> ## Spiritual engineers must be prepared to serve!

Preparing

We are *spiritual* engineers who must develop our minds (which are transformed through Christ). God's calling to preach is also a call to prepare. Preparation has *spiritual*, physical, emotional, and intellectual implications. As we go deeper, we are able to better understand and simplify our messages for those to whom God has called us.

Jesus did not stop with the simple commandment to *Love God*. He provided for an assisting command that is theologically non-negotiable. He indicates we are also mandated to "love people."

Truthfully, loving God is much more appealing than loving people. Some folks are easier to love than others. If we could pick and choose, then it would not be so bad. However, that option is not available in the heart of God. We must love all…even our enemies!

"…love your enemies, do [what is] good…expecting nothing in return… For He is gracious to the ungrateful and evil" (Luke 6:35).

> Guard and prepare physically, intellectually, emotionally, and spiritually!

Preaching

In regards to preaching, "People do not care how much you know, until they know how much you care." If there is contempt in the heart, it will overflow into the preaching. We have no option other than to love or we will preach with rebellion in our heart. Sooner or later what is on the inside will flow to the outside.

This lesson came early in my ministry. As I write this material, I have been in ministry over thirty-seven years. Throughout those many years, it would be most impressive to say that everybody was deeply in love with my leadership; however, that is not so. There have been many nights of anguish and discomfort. There have even been times when my life was threatened. Loving those people is most certainly difficult.

> Failure to love is NOT an option!

Many years ago, a deacon threatened me following Sunday morning worship. Without thinking, I quickly remarked, "Kyle (not his real name), I love you!" Even I was amazed when those words came out. Needless to say, this was not the last time, and I have not always been so *spiritual*. However, loving all is not an option!

> If God so loved the world, then where (or when) in the world am I not to do likewise?

Love the unlovely

How does one learn to love the unlovely? This goes back to developing the mind of Christ. Jesus is the only Authority whereby this can happen. As we pray for the unlovely, God will provide the love for our enemies—so be prepared! Enemies will appear, but God's grace is sufficient—"My grace is sufficient for you" (2 Corinthians 12:9). Sometimes we will find it necessary to preach to those people who are definitely unlovely, but they need our love—and we need to love them.

Love my neighbor

How, then, can we love our neighbor? First, one cannot stay in the study and love his neighbors. There must be contacts, communications, and meaningful encounters. Here is where preachers earn the right to be heard. There must be accessibility and transparency. The "preacher…congregation" relationship can never be "we…y'all" experience; it is an "us" experience. We are all together on this journey called life.

Secondly, love demands service. Preachers must remember that the Master Preacher was in the business of scratching where people itched. Jesus began His ministry in the Gospel of John with the words, "What seek ye?" (John 1:38, KJV).

True leaders are servants. Jesus said, "…whoever wants to become great among you must be your servant" (Matthew 20:26). It is amazing how badly strained relationships become great relationships when leaders dismiss the ego. One cannot love others and communicate a condescending spirit. The difference in the world's greatest preacher and the globe's vilest sinner is simply a relationship with Jesus Christ.

Jesus, said, "The Son of Man did not come to be served, but to serve, and to give His life—a ransom for many [friends and enemies]" (Matthew 20:28).

Conclusion

Preaching is not an exercise of speaking. Preaching is an exercise of communication, and it requires earning the right to be heard. The Apostle Paul tells young Timothy, "Be diligent to present yourself approved to God, a worker who doesn't need to be ashamed, correctly teaching the word of truth" (2 Timothy 2:15).

How do we accomplish this?

LOVE GOD!
LOVE PEOPLE!

CHAPTER 3

COMMITMENT

Proper Understanding
and Adherence to the Calling

S ince we have been called by God to proclaim His Word, we only have two options. A person can make all sorts of justifications and rationalized arguments, but in the end, we respond to our calling with a simple "Yes" or "No." God honors both answers. As a seminary student under the tutelage of Dr. Jack McGorman, I can still hear his words ringing, "God honors our 'no.'" The Psalmist writes:

> "But My people did not listen to Me; Israel did not obey Me.
> So I gave them over to their stubborn hearts
> to follow their own plans" (Psalms 81:11-12).

Sovereign ~ Absolute Authority

The author understands the danger of some who will challenge the theological implications of what is about to be stated. There is neither the intent nor any desire to present anything that dilutes the sovereignty of God. You can rest assured, the God of the Bible is indeed sovereign! Having said that—now is the time to address something that shall never be explained: "The will of The Sovereign God is not always accomplished."

God is sovereign!

Somewhere in God's sovereignty (absolute authority), He has created a situation which cannot be addressed logically but nonetheless is true. Humans make choices. Even the "active" voice of Greek verbs in the New Testament represents "the subject as the doer or performer of the action."[5]

One biblical passage that clearly illustrates the fact that God's will is not always accomplished may be found in 2 Peter 3:9:

> "The Lord does not delay His promise, as some
> understand delay, but is patient with you, *not wanting*
> any to perish, but all to come to repentance."

The word for "wanting" (*boulomai*, KJV) means to "will deliberately, have a purpose, be minded."[6] In other words, if God has His way, every precious soul that has ever existed would spend eternity with Him in Heaven. However, the inerrant Word of God clearly indicates that only a few will ultimately spend eternity with God in glory. Matthew 7:14 offers, "Narrow is the gate and difficult the road that leads to life, and *few*[7] (*oligos*: a small number or quantity) find it."

---

5   Strong's Greek and Hebrew Dictionary.

6   Ibid.

7   Strong's Greek and Hebrew Dictionary.

Humans can and do say, "NO" to God. Christians say, "NO" to God. Yes, even preachers say, "NO" to God! *How?*

- **In the basic call to preach.** Just as Jonah sinned, preachers also sin. Sometimes God chooses to be persistent. Sometimes preachers continue to the point of God's release. "But My people did not listen to Me; Israel did not obey Me. So I gave them over to their *stubborn hearts* to follow their own plans" (Psalm 81:11-12).

- **After answering God's call, "NO" can follow in many ways.** *How?*
  - » By refusing to go where God calls;
  - » By refusing to preach on what God says;
  - » By failing to properly prepare messages and in one's own personal walk;
  - » By becoming so busy doing good things that one begins to rationalize lack of preparing and preaching;
  - » By not going when God calls (i.e., "Later, Lord").

"As they were traveling on the road someone said to Him, 'I will follow You wherever You go!' Jesus told him, 'Foxes have dens, and birds of the sky have nests, but the Son of Man has no place to lay His head.' Then He said to another, 'Follow Me.' 'Lord,' he said, 'first let me go bury my father.' But He told him, 'Let the dead bury their own dead, but you go and spread the news of the kingdom of God.' Another also said, 'I will follow You, Lord, but first let me go and say good-bye to those at my house.' But Jesus said to him, 'No one who puts his hand to the plow and looks back is fit for the kingdom of God'" (Luke 9:57-62).

God's preachers must not only say, "YES" to the call on the front end, but we must also continue daily. The road may be long and the midnight oil may need to burn, but the Apostle Paul admonishes us with encouragement:

> "So we must not get tired of doing good, for we will reap
> at the proper time if we don't give up" (Galatians 6:9).

Commitment to the Call

Commitment to our calling is not always easy. Paul knew his young preacher boy, Timothy, would have moments when sharing God's Word would either be difficult or dangerous. In no uncertain terms he says, "I solemnly charge you: proclaim the message; persist in it whether convenient or not" (2 Timothy 4:1-2).

This is neither a suggestion nor a good idea. The word "charge"—solemnly charge—is *diamarturomai*. That word is made of a prefix (*dia*) and a root word (*martureo*). The English translation of "charge" is "to impose a task or responsibility on someone"[8] The Greek prefix, *dia*, means "through." The root *martureo* yields "to affirm that one has seen, heard, or experienced something." This combination brings about urgency in the message of Paul to young Timothy. There is a firmness that suggests that this message is not an option. The urgency is obvious.

Why spend so much time on "commitment" to God's call on one's life, especially a preacher's? The answer is simple—too many men are bailing out for various reasons. Excuses include moral failure, lack of support, timidity, and difficulties which arise while proclaiming truth to a culture that disconnects absolutes. Many reports of preachers leaving the ministry exist, but it is seldom mentioned that these men are also leaving God's call and purpose.

What, then, can be done? How can we assure ourselves that we will not become a statistic, and we will stay until the final trumpet sounds?

---

8   Merriam-Webster Online Dictionary.

Resoluteness

One word comes to mind that is seldom used in modern secularistic culture. It is the word "resolve." This word is defined by Merriam-Webster as "fixity of purpose: resoluteness." The word, "resoluteness" is defined as "marked by firm determination, bold, steady."

> **The one thing that keeps many in the saddle is a commitment to the calling!**

There will be occasions when the difficulty of proclaiming God's Word will be challenging. No matter what happens, obedience to God's call must be the order of the day. Preachers ought to predetermine that early in ministry. Obedience will reduce the stress that comes with decision making. There is never any other option.

One biblical character who became challenged in his walk with God was the prophet Daniel. In Daniel 1:8 the Bible says, "Daniel determined that he would not defile himself." The King James Version says, "But Daniel purposed in his heart." There was already an internal decision that precluded anything that might have become a circumstantial challenge.

Preachers would do well to "purpose in their hearts." This way, regardless of opposition, there is a definite resolve that brings strength and confidence. There is no guesswork. The decision has already been made.

Satan will not leave God's messengers alone. The lure of fame, ease, fortune, and popularity will cross the path of God's preachers. Not long after seminary, I was invited to participate in a business opportunity that would greatly enhance my financial position. This crossroad was simple to navigate. I had already "purposed in my heart" to serve the Lord no matter what. The result and decision was obvious: THE MASTER over money.

Jesus' Declaration

Luke 2:49b offers a simple, yet powerful synopsis of Jesus' commitment to Kingdom priority. He remarked, "Didn't you know that *I had to* be in my Father's house?" The following verse (v 50) says, "But they did not understand."

While the King James translates verse 49 as "My Father's business," there is no distortion of what Jesus meant. The key is found in the phrase "I had to" or "I must." The Greek word *dei* is from the root *deo* which signifies "binding" or "being fastened" to something. There can be no separation of Jesus and the business of the Father's Kingdom. Jesus was resolute even at twelve years of age (v 42).

God is faithful!

Romans 8:38-39 states that absolutely nothing shall have the power to separate us from the love of God that is in Christ Jesus our Lord! Why? God is faithful! He is committed to us in that He died for us. He simply desires that we live for Him.

We, too, then shall be "bound" or "fastened" to His calling on our lives. We must allow the bond of God's Holy Spirit to be *spiritual superglue*. Sometimes we will find that a genuine commitment to the calling will be the only thing that keeps us going. It may not make any sense. It did not when Jesus demonstrated it ("They did not understand"), and it probably will not make sense to many of us—but we must keep on keeping on. Job said, "Even if He kills me, I will hope in Him. I will still defend my ways before Him" (Job 13:15).

Being About the Father's Business

The bottom line for "being about the Father's business" is maintaining focus and staying on top of what God has called us to do. There will be many distractions. Those distractions may not always be something that is bad, but rather good things that still are not the best. We should never allow good things to keep us from the best things. We must always allow "good" to be defined in terms of our basic calling.

The preacher must maintain focus!

A classic text on this very issue is found in Acts 6. The people needed attention. They had issues with the pastors. A decision had to be made. In these verses we find how they were able to remedy the conflict of time and energy. One must remember they were dealing with thousands of people. They already had pastoral experience and ministry capital invested in the lives of these people. This is demonstrated by the content of the following passage:

> "In those days, as the **number** of the disciples **was multiplying**, there arose a complaint by the Hellenistic Jews against the Hebraic Jews that their widows were being overlooked in the daily distribution. The **twelve** summoned the whole company of the disciples and said, 'It would not be right for us to give up preaching about God to wait on tables'" (Acts 6:1-2).

The Bible says, "The number of the disciples was multiplying." *Why?*

Two reasons:

- o The disciples were ministering to the practical needs of the people.
- o The disciples were proclaiming the truth of God to the people.

Being About My Father's Business…Opportunities

o   The more people, the more challenges. The fact that they were growing is a sign that God was providing great opportunity. This opportunity allowed not only for numerical growth, but also growth in the *spiritual* and organizational skills of the early church's leaders.

Being About My Father's Business…Obstacles

o   "You can tell the size of a man by what it takes to stop him."[9]

o   "If you do not meet the devil head on, you are probably going his way."[10] We should feel honored that Satan thinks enough of us to attempt to block what we are doing.[11] We must keep going.

Being About My Father's Business…Obligation

Get connected and remain connected to God. It would not be right for us to give up preaching. Sermons do not just fall from the sky. They require diligent prayer and study. Late Saturday evening messages must never be the norm.

o   Take time to pray.

o   Study and meditate.

o   Crave the things of God.

In a later chapter, we will discuss how to take this idea and apply it to relevant communication with modern culture.

---

9   Dr. Adrian Rogers, in a message preached at Bellevue Baptist Church in Memphis, Tennessee.

10   Dr. Jack Gray, Spiritual Foundations Class, Southwestern Baptist Theological Seminary in Fort Worth, Texas: 1978.

11   The first Christian martyr, Stephen, saw the glory of God even when the obstacles took his life. (Acts 7:54-60).

Being About My Father's Business...Organization

Organizing can be a preacher's greatest friend. However, it is often easier to do everything yourself. Here is a simple strategy to incorporate organization in one's leadership modus operandi that will actually enhance the preacher's effectiveness.

- o Develop a strategy.
- o Enlist people.
- o Train people.
- o Empower people to do it.

Organization...Friend? Or foe?

Egos are fed by pleasing people; however, the ministry will only grow as large as an individual *unless* others are incorporated into the process. The leaders of the first church were wise in the calling of the first deacons to administrate the tangible needs of the early believers. The result is that the pastors were able to focus. Scripture says, "But we will *devote* ourselves to prayer and to the preaching ministry" (Acts 6:4).

The word, "devote" (*proskartereo*) means to face steadfastness. Careful attention is the order of the day. There is no instant *spirituality* that yields some supernatural sermon from the throne room of the universe. The idea is that there is constant attention being given to the matter and calling of God. The Greek "voice" and "mood" of this word indicates that there is participation on the part of the preacher, and it is a simple statement of fact. In other words, there are no options. We must give ourselves to the hard work at hand.

To be devoted is to face steadfastness!

Pray and Proclaim

The two objects of our devotion are prayer and proclamation. There is a reason for that order:

- o Preaching without prayer is flat!
- o Prayer without proclamation is rebellion against the calling of God!

Dig and Deliver

The "ministry" (*diakonia*) of the Bible is one of interesting nuances. The designation is basically one where "a person executes the commands of others." In the case of preaching, we execute the command of God. It also, however, comes from a concept of preparing and presenting food for consumption. As that is applied to preaching, it means that we are to dig and deliver a message from the Word of God which is the *Bread of Life.*

Conclusion

A call to preach is a call to prepare.

Just as we would never deliver raw, uncooked meat or unprepared food to guests in our homes, *spiritual* nutrition is even more important. It is vital for God's preachers to labor in the galley of their study and offer a *spiritual* cuisine which has all of the nutrients for a balanced *spiritual* diet. There is no such thing as *spiritual* fast food or instant microwavable fare. We must also not go to our neighbor's cupboard and take what is theirs for our own.

Prepare...No Shortcuts!

God called us to *prepare*. That preparation comes from prayer and study.

Preach...Commitment!

God called us to *preach*. Preaching is a commitment.

CHAPTER 4

COMMISSION

Purpose and Mission

C ommissioned? Merriam-Webster defines *commission* as "a formal written warrant granting the power to perform various acts or duties." We preach because we have been CALLED and COMMISSIONED.

There is often confusion regarding the difference between PURPOSE and MISSION. While it is not simple, there is a definitive way to distinguish between the two:
  o The *Purpose Statement* gives the big picture of WHAT is expected.
  o The *Mission Statement* offers an overview of HOW the purpose will be accomplished.

For example, at Wallace Memorial Baptist Church, we have a purpose statement and a mission statement:
  o *Our Purpose* is to fulfill the great commission by winning and growing people for the glory of our Lord Jesus Christ!

    o   *Our Mission* is to Love God, Connect with People, and Impact the World!

It is the hope and prayer of our pastoral staff that every member of our church takes the *purpose* and *mission* statements seriously. Since we have begun to promote these in a more defined manner, we now have more people involved in mission and ministry projects. We also have more people committed to having a daily devotional time with the goal of *Reading Through the Bible In A Year*. The spiritual health of our church is being built on a solid foundation!

Attitude of Christ

In regards to purpose, every preacher ought to develop the same purpose as Christ. Philippians 2:5 says; "Make your own *attitude* that of Christ Jesus."

    o   Attitude has mental and emotional vantage points.

    o   Cherish the same views as Christ.

His Spirit must be my (your) spirit. His passion must be my (your) passion. His purpose must be my (your) purpose. His mission must be my (your) mission. *Why?* Certainly not so we will receive human applause. The Apostle Paul aptly wrote: "Therefore, whether you eat or drink, or whatever you do, do everything for God's glory" (1 Corinthians 10:31). And my dear friend, that includes preaching!

Seek and Save

The purpose of Christ is succinctly established in His own words: "For the Son of Man has come to *seek* and to *save* the lost" (Luke 19:10).

Our purpose, then, is to "seek" and "save"—that is, seek the lost and lead them toward salvation in Jesus. Therefore, the crux of our preaching must keep this purpose in mind. We must go…go wherever the people are physically, spiritually, emotionally, and mentally. Seeking out folks is the *modus operandi* of Jesus. He met them wherever they were—physically, spiritually, emotionally, and mentally—and then, He walked with them to wherever they needed to be. That was what Jesus did!

The Holy Spirit does the work!

The saving part must be left with the Holy Spirit. We can only offer opportunity for salvation. God must do the work. It is spiritual in nature and cannot be coerced. Our job is to offer every opportunity and provide for an atmosphere conducive to saying "yes" to Jesus, but only God can save.

The Great Commission

There is not only one *Great Commission*. Indeed, there is one in each of the gospels and one in Acts. These may be found in the following passages:

Matthew 28:16-20 – "The 11 disciples traveled to Galilee, to the mountain where Jesus had directed them. When they saw Him, they worshiped, but some doubted. Then Jesus came near and said to them, 'All *authority* has been given to Me in heaven and on earth. Go, therefore, and make disciples of all nations, baptizing them in the name of the Father and of the Son and of the Holy Spirit, teaching them to observe everything I have commanded you. And remember, I am with you always, to the end of the age.'"

Mark 16:15 – "Then He said to them, 'Go into all the world and *preach* the gospel to the whole creation.'"

Luke 24:48 – "*You are witnesses* of these things."

John 20:21 – "Jesus said to them again, 'Peace to you! As the Father has sent Me, *I also send you.*'"

Acts 1:8 – "But you will receive power when the Holy Spirit has come upon you, and *you will be My witnesses* in Jerusalem, in all Judea and Samaria, and to the ends of the earth."

The remainder of this chapter will deal with the practical and theological implications of these passages as they relate to preaching.

Leadership Summit

One of the last things done by Jesus prior to His ascension was to meet with the remaining eleven disciples in Galilee. Matthew 28:16 reveals that Jesus had predetermined the meeting place:

- o HCSB: "The eleven disciples traveled to Galilee, to the mountain where *Jesus had directed them.*"
- o KJV: "Then the eleven disciples went away into Galilee, into a mountain where *Jesus had appointed them.*"

There are several subtle nuances in this passage that are devotional in nature and practical in application. The "commission" is obviously the main point, but one should not overlook other truths found in this account.

The Journey

First, the "eleven disciples traveled" (Matthew 28:16). The King James' "went away" rightly describes one element of the Greek word *poreuomai*. In this case the disciples left the bustle of Jerusalem with all of the resurrection conflict and journeyed to the slower-paced Galilee. The devotional truth is this: we cannot stay in the fray all of the time and be effective in the mission to which God has called us. The old time preacher said, "We must come apart lest we come—apart." Jesus wanted to meet with them in private.

Secondly, the word indicates that there are lessons being learned on the journey. Why did Jesus not just meet them on the Mount of Olives? It would have been much closer.

Perhaps His desire was for them to talk about their experiences of recent days. This would be an excellent time to debrief. The 100-mile journey of walking certainly included grieving and reflecting on all that Jesus had said and done. The point is that we must always be reflecting on our experiences with God. Too often we get so focused on the destination that we forget the journey. Do not miss the journey!

Thirdly, they were on the move. There was no virtual tour. The journey was the real thing. It required nourishment, refreshment, and rest; however, they were on the move!

You cannot be an effective communicator of biblical truth and remain still. Someone said, "God directs moving objects." Sitting and waiting for opportunity is a death knoll to any Christian worker. One must get up and go to the fields. They are "white already to harvest" (John 4:35, KJV).

Early in my ministry I was called to the Boulevard Baptist Church in Memphis, Tennessee. There was a gentleman on staff in a part-time position. When I first met with him in his office, he asked to see the bottom of my shoes. To my embarrassment, there was a hole in the sole. When he saw it, he abruptly said, "Anyone with a hole in the sole of his shoes can be my pastor." He was a retired pastor, and I was a young pastor in my late twenties. He was communicating that the church did not need a C.E.O. It needed a worker who was on the go.

Vision comes from God!

Where there is no vision, the people perish (Proverbs 29:18, KJV).

The vision is the destination; it comes from God. Preachers must seek God's destination for His people and clearly articulate that destination. In other words, one cannot simply be on the move. (Caution: There can be countless activity but very little direction.) Preachers must go to the place God directs. The disciples were headed to the mountain where Jesus had directed.

Interestingly many significant biblical events took place in the mountains:

- o   Abraham offered Isaac;
- o   God spoke in the burning bush;
- o   The giving of The Ten Commandments;
- o   Elijah and Mt. Carmel;
- o   The arrest on Olivet;
- o   The respite for Jesus (Caesarea Phillipi);
- o   The Crucifixion;
- o   The Ascension;
- o   even The Second Coming.

These are all only a sampling of significant events connected with mountains. One constant is that for the most part, this is where God could speak without the noise of life cluttering the ears and minds of His servants. Everyone needs a place where God can speak. When the proverbial preaching well runs dry (and it sometimes will), God's servant ought to heed the advice of the Psalmist:

> "I raise my eyes toward the mountains.
> Where will my help come from?
> My help come from the LORD" (Psalms 121:1-2a).

When Leaders See Jesus

There were two basic responses of the eleven upon their arrival. It was there that they *saw Him*. One cannot look upon our Lord without responding. Let it not go unnoticed that these were the foundational pillars upon which the church would be built. When these leaders came into contact with the risen Lord, they were either *delighted* or *doubtful*.

Delight

The element of delight expresses itself in worship. The word, *proskuneo*, indicates positioning one's self *spiritually*, emotionally, and physically below the one being honored. To "worship" means to bow and kiss the hand as a sign of servitude. Strong's Concordance equates this to "a dog licking the hand of his master." This involves recognition of the elevated status of our Lord.

The word "reverence" must be included in any discussion of worship. "Fear" (as the translation of the Hebrew word used here) would not be altogether correct. Recognition of "awe" and "excellent grandeur" would be more appropriate.

Some misunderstand "reverence" as only being still. On the contrary, reverencing may include a large vocal celebration of the day and majesty of God. Sometimes it is appropriate to be quiet: "Be still, and know that I am God" (Psalms 46:10, KJV). Contextually, the Holman Bible indicates here that fighting had become a distraction. It is very difficult to know God's presence and power when there is relational unrest.

There is also a time to verbally and visually celebrate in worship. Psalm 47:1-2 clearly states, "Clap your hands, all you peoples; shout to God with a jubilant cry. For the LORD Most High is awe-inspiring, a great King over all the earth."

There is a delicate balance between sublime solitude and emotional expression. When one is excluded, genuine worship may be short changed.

o   There is a time to be quiet...
o   There is a time to proclaim...

Wisdom and spiritual discernment will assist in knowing the appropriate time to do both.

Doubt

"...but some *doubted.*" These were the leaders. These were witnesses to the resurrection! These were the ones who experienced sign after sign. But how could they... *Why were they doubting?*

> ## Even the best leaders have human elements!

Doubt (*distazo*) means "to have reservation or to waiver." The underlying concept of abandonment is present. There is an inconsistency that arises and causes internal turmoil. *Doubt* is antithetical to trust or confidence. The Aorist Greek tense indicates it is a point in time that is not necessarily repeated. It is what it is for that moment.

Even though this is not a good thing, it does indicate that even the best of leaders have weak moments. Regardless of the evidence, we all have times of anxiety and lack of trust. This is not so much an indication of our moral stature as it is our human nature.

When God calls *spiritual* leaders, they are still human. Never should that be an excuse for sin, but it can be an explanation for lack of strength. It is refreshing to know that God can and does use people who have doubts. *Spiritual* leaders cannot and must not allow the guilt that comes from doubt to paralyze one's willingness to continue in ministry.

There are even times when we must preach when the "feeling" is not there. We will feel unworthy (which is always the case), unprepared, ineffective, and downright distant from God. However, we must go on. As the Apostle Paul was mentoring his prize preacher boy, Timothy, he said, "... *proclaim the message; persist in it whether convenient or not*" (2

Timothy 4:2, HCSB). The King James says, *"Preach the word; be instant in season, out of season..."*

In other words, regardless of what may be going on internally or externally, we must continue to preach God's Word. Often, it is when we do not "feel like it" that God does His greatest work.

There is a story of a young preacher who had studied, prayed, and was truly ready to unload the arsenal of biblical truth on the congregation. He was pumped, primed, and ready. When time came, he proudly stood before the congregation. However, he soon realized that the message was uninspiring and ineffective. At the end of the service, his all-time "high" was replaced with a "gut-wrenching" low. Upon leaving, one sweet prayer warrior walked passed him and said, "If you had gone into the pulpit the way you walked out, you would have walked out the way you walked in."

What a great lesson! It is not about our persuasive words; it is God's Spirit. In 1 Corinthians 2:1-5, every preacher will find the biblical perspective on effectively communicating biblical truth:

> "When I came to you, brothers, announcing the testimony of God to you, I did not come with brilliance of speech or wisdom. For I determined to know nothing among you except Jesus Christ and Him crucified. And I was with you in *weakness*, in *fear*, and in *much trembling*. My speech and my proclamation were not with persuasive words of wisdom, but with a demonstration of the Spirit and power, so that your faith might not be based on men's wisdom but on God's power."

Here we find some "take a ways" from God's Word to give assurance that His truth is going forth.

- o "in weakness, in fear, and in much trembling...not with persuasive words...but with a demonstration of the Spirit."

- o The proof was made known not by human iniquity, but rather by God's Spirit.
- o The Apostle Paul wrote approximately half of the New Testament.

God honors our faithfulness to proclaim, even when accompanied by doubt and fear. His Word will be effective when proclaimed, regardless of how we feel. Isaiah 55:11 says, "so My word that comes from My mouth will not return to Me empty."

Authority

As Jesus opened His earthly ministry, there was a reference to His "authority." John 2:18 is a request for Jesus' credentials: "The Jews replied to Him, 'What sign [of authority] will You show us for doing these things?'"

Several issues are clarified:
1. The Issue of Authority.
   (*Exousia:* The jurisdiction to exercise management and control over people and situations) Jesus has the responsible right to determine who, what, and where. He is our Ultimate Authority. There is no higher power. Once His mandate is set into motion, there is no right to appeal. The reason this is important to the preacher is because some will say, "Who are you to tell me what to do?" Quite honestly, those who make such statements are correct! The preacher, in and of himself, has no more right than anyone else. However, when Jesus says something, He does have the right. This is why preachers ought to reduce comments such as "I think" and replace them with the words, "The Bible says..." The Bible is the authority!
2. The Issue of Authority's Expanse.

Where is the jurisdiction of Jesus' authority? The answer is "in heaven and on earth." That sums up the subjects of God's authority. There is no place to escape the power and control of God. Nobody is exempt.

3. The Range of Authority.

Jesus' authority is not limited to just matters of religious or spiritual issues. God has business in the market places, homes, personal relationships, schools, politics, and the list goes on to include any area of life imaginable. Modern culture has clouded the range of God's authority excluding Him from select places. Under the anti-biblical message of "separation of church and state,"[12] social interest anti-Christian groups have attempted to diminish the idea of God in politics and public life. Preachers must not be intimidated when the full council of God's Word is declared. It affects every area of human existence—All Authority!

Go Tell

All five of the commissioning passages reflect the idea of being commissioned by God to communicate the gospel throughout the entire world. There is little ambiguity regarding the message. Several affirming thoughts need to be kept in mind as God's messengers live out the Divine calling:

1. The indwelling Spirit of God (Acts 1:8) affords the preacher power to proclaim.

Apart from God's Spirit, man's preaching is in vain. We must all recognize that upon receiving Christ as Lord and Savior, we not only receive the gifts of the Spirit, we also receive the Gift of the Spirit: The Spirit Himself. He is the dynamite power in our lives that is able to transform hearts and lives. We are not given the Spirit to be containers, but rather conduits. He must flow through us.

---

12 This is not in the Constitution of the United States but in a letter written by Thomas Jefferson to the messengers of the Danbury Baptist Association in the state of Connecticut on January 1, 1802.

o   "...you will receive power when the Holy Spirit has come on you"

o   "power" → *dunamis* → dynamite

Not IF but rather WHEN!

2. The result of being *called* is being *sent* (John 20:21).
As the Father sent Jesus, He sends us. We are sent for the same purpose: "to seek and save the lost" (Luke 19:10). The bottom line of all preaching must be to introduce people to Christ and to assist them in growing in that relationship.
3. The preacher's vision must be the entire world (Matthew 28:18; Mark 16:15; Acts 1:8).
The church field does not end at 10th Street and Main. Every human being has the right to know of God's redeeming love. Too often preachers allow money, logistics, laziness, and many other factors to keep them from sensing a global *spiritual* responsibility. As this truth is kept in mind, preaching will be transformed and hearers will develop an "I can" mentality.

"Jesus came near and said...'All authority has been given to Me in heaven and on earth. Go, therefore, and make disciples of all nations... teaching them to observe everything I have commanded you. And remember, I am with you always'" (Matthew 28:18-20).

4. Much has been made about "going" (Matthew, Mark) being a participle.

That would indicate "going" is assumed. It is not "if" but rather "when" you go. In other words, sharing the truths must move from being an event that happens at eleven o'clock on Sunday morning to an everyday lifestyle. The result of every biblical message ought to be to "win" and "grow" people. People who do not know God through Christ ought to be clearly made aware of how that can change. People who are followers of Christ ought to be challenged to move further along in their *spiritual* journey—which is "baptizing" and "making disciples."

Conclusion

While the word "missions" is not in the biblical text, the mission is all over it:

o   The commissioning is an authorization to represent Him by proclaiming His Word to people everywhere— anything less is disobedience!

o   Every sermon rightly prepared, prayed over, and delivered with humility and awe is not only a fulfillment, it is fulfilling!

"I have spoken; yes, I have called him; I have brought him, and he will succeed in his mission" (Isaiah 48:15).

God-called preachers are commissioned by God!

CHAPTER 5

CONTENT

Theme

J ESUS... Proclaim Him! Preach Him! The Bible charges us in 2 Timothy 4:2 to "...proclaim the message; persist in it whether convenient or not" (HCSB) and "Preach the word; be instant in season, out of season" (KJV).

Knowing the context, one can gain much knowledge about people by listening to the words of music that is written and sung. Music is like a window to the soul. It affords access to the thoughts, ideas, dreams, and even heartaches of people. An entire biblical book (*Psalms*) is a compilation of songs that describes the author (whom I believe to be primarily King David) in his relationship with God. In the *Psalms* are both human hurts and hope. In them are both misery and majesty. The theology included is vast and meaningful.

Twenty-first Century *spiritual* music is not unlike the *Psalms*. There are simple truths accompanied by deep theology. Because the human experience is varied, so are musical expressions. In all that is sung, one theme should resonate in every biblically accurate musical expression: Jesus Christ.

Christo-Centric Preaching

This central theme of *JESUS* does not begin with adulthood. A catchy song which became popular with children in the mid-1900s said:

> "Jesus, Jesus,
> Jesus in the morning,
> Jesus in the noontime,
> Jesus, Jesus,
> Jesus when the sun goes down."[13]

In this entire verse there are 18 words, and approximately one-third of those words are the same: *Jesus*. Whatever the song may say to the listener, the theme is *Jesus*. Taking into account the logical progression and meaning behind the text, one hears the singer calling for a continual recognition and communication with Jesus during every waking moment. There is a technical theological term that describes this: *Christo-centric*. Basically, it says that Christ is the central theme of the song.

> "...so that He might come to have first place in everything" (Colossians 1:18).

Biblical preaching has the same underlying theme. The axis upon which every biblical message rotates is Jesus Christ. Regardless of Old

---

13   Title: "Jesus, Jesus, Jesus in the Morning." Source: The musical tune is an American folk song while the lyrics are attributed to African-American folk lore.

Testament or New Testament, Jesus must be the focus. Regardless of topic, Jesus must be the center. Technically and biblically speaking, preaching has not occurred unless it is *Christo-centric*. Tangent messages are dangerous. Everything must come back to Christ.

The church at Corinth was made aware of this quickly in Paul's first letter. The reason we know more about the Corinthian church than any other in the New Testament is because of their many problems. Most of the issues arose because they were preoccupied with numerous worldly concerns. The church had removed Christ from the center of ministry and replaced Him with various subjects, issues, philosophies, and arguments. That is why Paul opened the letter with some nice greetings (1 Corinthians 1:1-9), acknowledged their troubles (v. 10-17), and then brought everything back into its proper focus (v. 18-25). The major key to solving the Corinthian church's problems is clearly articulated in the first part of verse 23, "but we preach Christ crucified." One of the most effective techniques to reel in wayward Christians is to bring them back to the basics.

One of my favorite illustrations regarding this came from Vince Lombardi. This professional football coach made a memorable half-time speech to his players. The team had come apart during the first half, and the result was confusion. Instead of team-spirited players, there were eleven individuals doing their own thing. It was no wonder they were down significantly at half-time. The coach stood in silence, held up a football and said, "Gentlemen, we must come back to the basics. This is a football." After other choice words, the coach sent the team out to play the second half, and they won the game.

Paul did the same thing in Corinth. Gentlemen, "We preach Christ crucified." In other words, it is time to return the centerpiece of our ministry to the core of our focus and activity:

We preach Christ crucified.

Preach Christ Crucified

There are four foundational pillars that constitute the content of *Christo-centric* preaching:

1. Association
2. Acclamation
3. Anointed
4. Atonement

Every biblical messenger must understand the nature of Paul's statement in order to adequately be an ambassador for God in the pulpit.

1. Association: "We"

"No man is an island entire of itself; every man is a piece of the continent, a part of the main..." —John Donne (1572-1631).

We is a first person plural pronoun meaning that the speaker is not alone. There are others included and engaged in this process. The Greek word *hemeis* is plural. *We* are better *together*!

Relationship

Relationship is why humans were created. We were formed to relate to God and to one another. It is not a part of God's plan for us to live in isolation. John Donne's quote "no man is an island" is biblically sound. God has not called us to be hermits, but helpers.

As Jesus developed the foundation of what would become the church, He did so with a group. Certainly there were individual times when our Lord mentored one disciple apart from the others, but most of the training was in the group.

"Iron sharpens iron, and one man sharpens another" (Proverbs 27:17).

Refinement

Preachers being trained in groups yield great opportunity for instruction and refinement. With Christ as the Master Teacher, life lessons can be communicated in word and deed. As Jesus imparts truth, questions arise. When individuals inquire, all benefit from His answer.

Working together with Jesus also keeps the focus on His priorities. The adage "WWJD" (*What Would Jesus Do?*) brings light on what is important to Him. Watching Jesus interact in the lives of others can bring important life lessons. Also, others may learn from how He interacts with us.

The foundational element of relationships is vital to *Christo-centric* preaching. As we all draw closer to Him, we become closer to one another. Being closer to one another provides strength. As one preacher said, "we are better together."

Respect

There may be times to sever ties, but do not burn bridges. For example, Paul and Barnabas—Acts 15:39 says, "There was such a sharp disagreement that they parted company." However, some scholars note that Paul still had respect for Barnabas. Preachers can (and will) disagree; however, we should strive to be agreeable. Respect does not mean we accept all that one says or does. It indicates a godly attitude demonstrated even during times of differences.

Responsibility

Prayer ~ One of my first experiences of prayerful encouragement was when a preacher whom I did not know at the time offered a prayer for me. Preachers praying for preachers offer strength that keeps us focused on Christ.

Praise ~ Encourage one another. Only preachers (and their spouses) can truly understand what other preachers are going through. We have a responsibility to encourage them, hold them accountable, and help build them up for the glory of Christ.

Problematic ~ When one falls, it affects all of us. In the late 1980s and early 1990s, there were several famous television preachers who failed morally and ethically. Not surprisingly, the secular media had a feeding frenzy. The result was that people began to look at all preachers with a skeptical eye. The up-side of this is that it called for all in the ministry to be assured that their house was in order. The down-side is that there are imperfections in every human. With communication and information being so readily available, any blemish can be magnified. Someone once said, "Any goose can be cooked with propaganda." We have a responsibility to *Walk the Walk* as well as *Talk the Talk*.

2. Acclamation: "we preach"

"...a loud eager expression of approval or praise...an overwhelming affirming vote by cheers, shouts..."[14]

When the Apostle Paul says, "we preach," there is a strong, unapologetic declaration of something that is held to be true, dear, and reliable. There is no holding back. The word *kerusso* indicates something is being published and proclaimed openly (Greek Strong's). There is a compulsion to communicate. The New International Version of Jeremiah 20:9 expresses the thrust of this word:

"But if I say, 'I will not mention Him or speak any more in His name,' His word is in my heart like a fire, a fire shut up in my bones. I am weary of holding it in; indeed, I cannot."

---

14 Merriam-Webster Online Dictionary.

The early church also had the same problem. Even when mandated by the authorities, they jeopardized physical comfort and security. The writer of Acts describes it thusly:

"They called in the apostles and had them flogged, they ordered them not to speak in the name of Jesus and released them. Then they went out from the presence of the Sanhedrin, rejoicing that they were counted worthy to be dishonored on behalf of the name. Every day in the temple complex, and in various homes, they *continued teaching and proclaiming* the good news that the Messiah is Jesus" (Acts 5:40-42).

> **All that is necessary for evil to triumph is for good men to do nothing!** —Edmund Burke[15]

God's preachers must preach...regardless. There is no room for wishy-washy, namby-pamby, feel-good spiritual talks. If there is a call to preach, PREACH! There is no need to back up or shut up. God has called His preachers to stand up—bridging the gap between the human and Divine. In Ezekiel 22:30, God is looking for one to "stand in the gap." The purpose was to protect the land from destruction, but tragically, no one rose to the occasion.

Preaching is not always a popular exercise. Indeed, biblical preachers often find themselves in the crossfire of a godless culture. However, there is no room for preachers to be ashamed of the gospel.

Over the years, the gospel has been tagged as a slaughterhouse or blood thirsty religion or a crutch for the weak. In many ways, it has become popular to be on the "anti-Christian" band wagon. (One

---

15 Quote cannot be definitely traced to either man, but most often it is attributed to Edmund Burke (1729-1797) but sometimes to John Philpot Curran (1750-1817).

church even forbade the preacher to preach about the cross or sing songs which mention the blood.)

A country singer popularized a song that said, "I was country when country wasn't cool." Well, we must be Christian even when "being Christian" is not cool. Though we may stand alone, we must declare with the Apostle Paul:

"For I am not ashamed of the gospel, because it is God's power for salvation to everyone who believes" (Romans 1:16).

Empowers

God empowers preachers to proclaim His message, even in the face of adversity: "God has not given us a spirit of fearfulness, but one of power (*dunamis*), love (*agape*), and sound judgment (*sophronismos*)" (2 Timothy 1:7); therefore, we need not fear anything or anyone aside from the Lord.

The story is told of Christians gathering one evening for a clandestine meeting. The location was in an undisclosed area in the heart of the Communistic Soviet Union. Having visited some of these "prayer houses," my mind can envision this setting:

While the Christian brothers were worshiping, KGB[16] agents stormed in and held the congregation at gunpoint. The Commander ordered, "If you will denounce your god, you may leave now and live!" As expected, some did. A second time the Commander offered those still remaining the same opportunity to live. A few more filtered out. And then a third and final time, he shouted the offer, but no one budged. Those remaining were now ready to face death for the Lord they loved. Unexpectedly, the soldiers laid down

---

16   KGB was the communistic national security agency of the Soviet Union from 1954 until 1991.

their weapons and joined those remaining in prayer. They explained that they could not chance being caught or turned in by marginal Christians.

> We must not be timid or afraid.
> The world is looking for what is real.

3. Anointed: "we preach **Christ**"

Christ is the direct object of this sentence. By definition, a "direct object" is "a word or phrase denoting the goal or the result of the action of a verb" (Webster's). The Apostle Paul is very succinct in describing the objective of his preaching: Christ!

The depth of Paul's assertion is pregnant with meaning. Christ is not the last name of Jesus. Christ is His title. Actually, Christ is a Greek translation of the Hebrew word Messiah. In order to understand Jesus as the Christ, a basic knowledge of the Hebraic "Messiah" is necessary. The word "Messiah" means "anointed one." Jeremiah thought God would make the selection of the Messiah!

A first attribute is that the Messiah would be installed into an office or position. This was not by chance. God specifically and purposefully made the assignment.

Secondly, this appointment has purpose. The king is not installed simply to perform the duties of the king. He is strategically placed by Divine design for a specified purpose, and that purpose would be to "execute a divinely appointed task" (Holman Dictionary).

Thirdly, the anointed one is God's representative. The action and voice of the Messiah are the actions and voice of God. Any response on behalf of humans is a response to God.

In Jewish thought, the Messiah would be a son of David (son being descendant). He would be a "warrior-prince who would expel the hated

Romans from Israel and bring in a kingdom in which the Jews would be promoted to world dominion" (Holman Bible Dictionary).

After the rebellion and overthrow of Israel, the cry for and expectation of the Messiah's arrival became even more prominent. The hope of the Jewish people was for a Savior of the world who would be appointed of God to bring forgiveness, peace, and prosperity. Every Jewish woman dreamed that she would become the maternal vessel that God would use to deliver this Messiah.

Jesus being the Messiah was vividly debated in the First Century. Undeniably, Jesus did not fit the mold of everyone's expectation. However, make no mistake about it, in Jesus' dialogue with Peter at Caesarea Philippi, the point is made clear. History's Messiah had come. Listen to the dialogue from Matthew 16:13-17:

> "When Jesus came to the region of Caesarea Philippi, He asked His disciples, 'Who do people say that the Son of Man is?'
>
> And they said, 'Some say John the Baptist; others, Elijah; still others, Jeremiah or one of the prophets.'
>
> 'But you,' He asked them, 'who do you say that I am?'
>
> Simon Peter answered, 'You are the Messiah, the Son of the living God!'
>
> And Jesus responded, 'Simon son of Jonah, you are blessed because flesh and blood did not reveal this to you, but My Father in heaven.'"

The text speaks for itself. Our message must be that Jesus is the Messiah. He is the Savior of the world. Regardless of what life-subject is being proclaimed by a preacher, everything must come back to this truth:

- o   Jesus is God!
- o   Jesus is the Messiah!
- o   Jesus is the Savior of the world!

4. Atonement: "we preach Christ **crucified**"

1 Corinthians 15:3-4 says, "Christ died for our sins according to the Scriptures, that He was buried, that He was raised on the third day according to the Scriptures."

The death of the Messiah was payment for the world's transgressions. It is on the cross that the payment is finalized. Preaching the atonement of Jesus is where forgiveness and peace may be found. The resurrection was not in doubt. The First Century Christians went to their death because they experienced the resurrection power and presence of Christ.

The crucifixion, however, had to be explained. Hebrews 9:22 clarified what every sincere Jew understood, "...without the shedding of blood there is no forgiveness."

Preaching the "crucified Christ" is the declaration of how humans can experience peace, hope, and forgiveness. The atonement is made by Jesus on our behalf. He was anointed to atone.

Conclusion

The Bible is filled with godly perspectives on many life issues. Everything from business, interpersonal relationships, marriage, church life, leadership, employment, as well as other issues and responsibilities are addressed by God's Word. However, one must never forget that every issue in the Bible rotates on the axis of Jesus Christ.

Regardless of the subject matter, the preacher must be constantly aware of Jesus. He is the adhesive that brings all of life together. In Corinth, the problems were numerous. It is no accident that the author began addressing all of those issues in the "Alpha and Omega, the First and the Last, the Beginning and the End" (Revelation 22:13).

Biblical preaching is Christo-centric preaching!

CHAPTER 6

CULTURE

Cultural Exegesis

The Bible is not only a book about God; it is a book about people. The Bible is a revelation of God's understanding and will for the people whom He loves. Ultimately, He offered His Son as a sacrificial substitution for their sins.

> "There is an occasion for everything,
> and a time for every activity
> under heaven" (Ecclesiastes 3:1).

The Hebrew term for "*occasion*" lends itself to communicating a situation or a moment. There are various things that converge to make something appropriate. The culture is ripe for certain activities. A wise biblical communicator understands the "occasion." This is where the people are living, thinking, and performing. This is what is on their hearts and minds.

Someone has rightly said, "We do not simply teach the Bible; we teach people the Bible." The underlying thought is that we must properly understand where people are in their intellectual, physical, emotional, and spiritual journeys. Failure to do so may produce sound biblical exposition which may be unintelligible to the audience.

An understanding of addressing people where they "are" is biblically sound. Many scriptural scholars are very astute in biblical studies, but they have no concept of how to relate spiritual truths to the practical needs of people. In other words, it is not enough to do sound biblical exegesis. One must also do sound cultural exegesis.

Exegesis [ek-si-**jee**-sis] is a word that every Bible preacher needs to know and understand. The most basic preaching classes properly teach that the soundest preaching comes from sound exposition. Expository preaching is "a discourse that is designed to convey information or explain something difficult to understand" (like the Bible). Proper exposition comes from proper exegesis. Exegesis is a word that technically means "to lead out from." In other words, you must go deep into the subject and bring out the real meaning. Exegeting culture is equally as important as exegeting scripture. It is not enough for a preacher to render an opinion on what "he thinks" may be the heartfelt issues of listeners. There needs to be a thorough investigation and understanding regarding where people are living:

» *What are the people thinking or experiencing?*
» *What are their goals and aspirations?*
» *What are their hang-ups and hurts?*
» *What occupies their attention?*

The importance of understanding culture is well-demonstrated all throughout the Bible. One vivid and simple example is found in 1 Corinthians 13:11:

"When I was a child, I spoke like a child, I thought like a child, I reasoned like a child. When I became a man, I put aside childish things."

The whole point of this statement is that where people find themselves in life will determine what they are able to handle. A thick filet mignon steak is no doubt a culinary delight that most hungry adults would welcome at meal time. However, a newborn babe would never be able to receive and digest a tender morsel of Angus delight. An attentive parent knows what the child can handle and then selects the meal accordingly. The same is true in proclamation. The preacher needs to evaluate his audience. This will enhance the effectiveness of the sermon.

After preaching on a particular issue one Sunday morning, a person from the congregation commented, "Preacher, you have been reading my mail." Obviously taken back by that comment, I replied, "Excuse me! Could you explain?" He responded, "Everything you talked about today is exactly where I am in life. You preached that sermon for me!"

I truly had no knowledge of what was going on with the gentleman, but what he was saying indicated that whatever was addressed in the sermon vividly hit home with his life experience.

- o Question: *Was this accidental or was it by design?*
- o Answer: What may seem to be accidental with us is by design with God. This, however, does not excuse us from attempting to discern what is happening in the lives of our listeners.

Encounter

> ### COMPONENTS IN EXEGETING CULTURE
> - Be with the people
> - Understand the pool you fish in
> - Maximize opportunities for ministry
> - Exercise spiritual discernment

1. Be with the people

I learned early in ministry that one cannot pastor people with an absentee relationship. Young people use a term that is biblical in scope—"Hang Out."

Where might Jesus hang-out? Possibly at campfires, journeys to the next town, synagogues, festivals, seashore… Jesus was personally involved in the lives of people. An example of Jesus' model is found in Matthew 8:14-15:

> "When *Jesus went* into Peter's house, *He saw* his mother-in-law lying in bed with a fever. So *He touched* her hand, and the fever left her. Then she got up and began to serve Him."

THE NATURE OF JESUS' WORKING
(Five Point Outline)

He came.	PRESENCE
He saw.	PERCEPTION
He touched.	POWER
He healed.	PERFORMANCE
She served.	PRAISE

One can easily see the result—the woman served Jesus. That ought to be the aim of our messages. The last point would never have been a reality if it were not for the first point: "He went." *Jesus went* where the people were. The religious or social status of the people was a non-issue. Jesus dialogued with professors, Pharisees, peasants, and prostitutes.

Then Jesus looked. The Bible says that He saw Peter's sick mother-in-law. He was aware of her hurts and needs. Her ailment became the vehicle by which Jesus would do a work in her life.

Spiritually successful preachers cannot make a genuine impact without being with people. As previously discussed, loving people is important to God. Love requires time, attention, and presence. Preachers ought to be personally involved with congregants (when doable). Those relationships will produce insight and rapport. If the preacher's job is to move people from where they are to where they are supposed to be, then the preacher needs to know where those people are. Being present with people offers a tremendous advantage. As one old preacher declared, "get out of the study and on to the sidewalk."

2. Understand the pool you fish in

My father-in-law is an avid fisherman. He once took me brim fishing. We were getting only a few nibbles. However, bass were jumping all around the boat. The problem was that we did not have gear to bass fish. If you are going to be a fisher of men, you need to understand the nature of the man you are trying to reach. You will be surprised as to how important this is.

Being a graduate of Southwestern Seminary in Fort Worth, Texas, I became an avid fan of Coach Tom Landry and the Dallas Cowboys. I was preaching in another state and was using an illustration to denote disappointments of life. I made a statement that indicated some particular situation would be as disappointing as having a Super Bowl without the Dallas Cowboys. A woman shouted out, "Why don't you just go back to Texas?" Whoops!

Different communities have different customs. They may not be right or wrong, just different. What may be offensive in one town may be seen as harmless in another. It is good to know idiosyncrasies. This helps the preacher from getting a common disease—foot-in-mouth.

Jesus knew the passions of the people He addressed. While this will be discussed in more detail in the section on communication and illustrations, Jesus used what the people knew and understood to illustrate kingdom principles. The most famous device implemented by our Lord is the Parable. This, too, will be addressed more fully in a later section as well; however, there are several examples worth noting:

> *Agriculture* ~ When Jesus spoke to people in rural areas of Galilee, He talked about sheep, farming, and family. The people understood those concepts.
>
> *Maritime* ~ Much of Jesus' earthly ministry was centered near the Sea of Galilee. Fishermen understood storms, nets, and catching fish. Jesus spoke their language.
>
> *Intellect* ~ When Jesus addressed educated people, He could "hold His own." Even at twelve years of age, He confounded scholars. Luke 2:47 says: "And all those who heard Him were astounded at His understanding and His answers."

This is not to say that all preachers must be intellectuals, but due diligence needs to be given to being well-read on a variety of subjects. Laziness is never an acceptable excuse!

The story is told of a young preacher who was bemoaning education. In his misplaced zeal, he confronted a well-respected seminary president and said, "God did not call me to be an intellectual!" Softly and with a statesman-like attitude the president responded, "...and God did not call me to be ignorant."

Preachers need to attempt to speak on the intellectual level of the hearers. This is not a technique designed to impress, but rather to enhance the glorious gospel of the Bible.

> *Politics* ~ All of my life I have heard, "You don't mix religion and politics." Oh really! *Why not?* The Bible certainly does. The political climate of Israel would rise and fall based on the spiritual integrity of the people. There is a direct tie between the national success and security of a people and their commitment to God. The entire Old Testament is a record of this very thing.

One of the major lies being promoted in America today is the notion that the church ought to stay out of any public agenda. Never does the Constitution of the United States assert that there should be separation of church and state. In context, the First Amendment is a reaction to the English government's official support of the Church of England. The First Amendment was written to protect churches, not restrict them.

The First Amendment guarantees Freedom of Religion. When the word "religion" was used in the time of our early national fathers, it meant denomination (*i.e.*, Baptist, Catholic, Presbyterian, etc.). It did not take into account global religions.

The problem today is that politicians have taken biblical moral concepts and built political platforms on them (*i.e.*, gay rights, abortion, etc.). Preachers are then told they must stay out of politics; therefore, they may not address these concepts. To do so would mean committing a hate crime that carries severe penalties.

The *Book of Acts* finds the early church in a similar situation. The authorities stated to those incarcerated, "Didn't we *strictly order you* not to teach in this name?" (Acts 5:28). They responded, "We must obey God rather than men" (Acts 5:29).

The secularists say to preachers, "You ought to mind your own business." Shockingly, I agree. The problem is that everything in this world is the business of God's preachers. The world may say, "No." God says, "Go!" Remember, it was the political structure that ultimately landed Jesus on the cross.

Evangelize

3. Maximize opportunities for ministry

Galatians 6:10 says: "Therefore, as we have opportunity, we must work for the good of all, especially for those who belong to the household of faith." The word for opportunity is *kairos* (time, situation, season). Ecclesiastes has already informed us that there is a "season" for everything. A spiritually gifted leader understands those seasons and maximizes kingdom effectiveness.

Even the coming of Christ happened when there were certain cultural alignments. The Bible states, "But when the completion of the time came, God sent His Son..." (Galatians 4:4). The "completion of the time" indicates that there were cultural things that had aligned which would maximize the advent of the Messiah. One scholar notes three important cultural developments that were in place at the time of Christ's birth:

Pax Romana ~ People were free to move about

Roman Roads ~ Enhanced spread of gospel

Greek Language ~ Precise documentation of the life of Jesus

While this may not be an exhaustive list, it certainly does indicate that there is a direct correlation between what is happening in the world and what God desires to do to enhance His kingdom. 2 Timothy 2:15 says we are to "rightly divide the word of truth." Good preachers are also adept at rightly dividing the world needing that truth.

The New International Version translates Ephesians 5:16-20 in a way that is clear and informative:

> "Be very careful, then, how you live—not as unwise but as wise, *making the most of every opportunity,* because the days are evil. Therefore do not be foolish, but understand what the Lord's will is...always giving thanks to God the Father for everything, in the name of our Lord Jesus Christ."

Simple common sense will sometimes offer assistance in "making the most of every opportunity." For example, Christmas is a time that, while not celebrated by everyone, is understood to be a Christian holiday. It is a golden "opportunity" to remind the world where it all began.

Even secular celebrations and holidays can be used. I was once asked where I thought Jesus would spend Super Bowl Sunday. My answer: "at the game." Jesus went to where the people were. He seized moments to communicate kingdom truth. Turning the water into grape juice (Baptist version) is a prime example of Jesus' presence and seizing the moment.

Engage

4. Exercise Spiritual Discernment

The ability to seize moments for maximizing *spiritual* communication begins with "spiritual discernment." Preachers must have this insight. This is the ability to read situations and understand them from God's perspective. The preacher must also have the biblical discernment to know how God responds and addresses these situations. The sermon is a bridge that connects people from the current situation to where God would desire them to be.

> ### "People without discernment
> ### are doomed" (Hosea 4:14).

Hosea underscores the importance of being able to read culture when he writes: "People without discernment are doomed" (Hosea 4:14). If this is so important, how is it defined? The Hebrew word means to "understand, know, and have the ability to read a situation."[17]

Where does spiritual discernment begin? Who is responsible for understanding and assessing it? Isaiah 56:11 says it is the shepherd's responsibility. Speaking of evil leaders who are condemned by God, the

---

17   Strong's.

prophet writes: "And they are shepherds who have no discernment…"
Without discernment, a shepherd could lead an entire herd into a pack
of wolves, and the destruction would be devastating.

Another prophetic illustration of this point is the concept of a
watchman. Ezekiel 33 shows the importance of the watchman being
alert and aware of potential danger. The watchman has the responsibility
to be on the lookout, know the enemy, see the enemy approaching,
and warn the people. Failure to do so will require retribution by God
on the one He made responsible. Listen to God as He describes this
illustration:

> "The word of the LORD came to me: 'Son of man, speak to
> your people and tell them: Suppose I bring the sword against
> a land, and the people of that land select a man from among
> them, appointing him as their watchman, and he sees the
> sword coming against the land and blows his trumpet to warn
> the people. Then, if anyone hears the sound of the trumpet
> but ignores the warning, and the sword comes and takes him
> away, his blood will be on his own head. [Since] he heard the
> sound of the trumpet but ignored the warning, his blood is on
> his own hands. If he had taken warning, he would have saved
> his life. However, if the watchman sees the sword coming but
> doesn't blow the trumpet, so that the people aren't warned,
> and the sword comes and takes away their lives, then they
> have been taken away because of their iniquity, but I will
> hold the watchman accountable for their blood. As for you,
> son of man, I have made you a watchman for the house of
> Israel…'" (Ezekiel 33:1-7).

If this is so vital to our effectiveness as spiritual leaders, and the
kingdom work is dependent on it, then how do we get "spiritual
discernment?" One thing is for sure, we do not come by it naturally.

God says, "For My thoughts are not your thoughts, and your ways are not My ways" (Isaiah 55:8). The Apostle Paul writes, "...the natural man does not welcome what comes from God's Spirit, because it is foolishness to him; he is not able to know it since it is evaluated spiritually" (1 Corinthians 2:14). The words, "evaluated spiritually" are rendered "spiritually discerned" in some translations.[18]

In other words, the preacher must allow the Holy Spirit to illuminate not only the Bible but the current culture. Jesus was teaching this to His disciples on the way to the cross. He instructed, "When the Spirit of truth comes, He will guide you into all the truth" (John 16:13). We must allow God's Spirit to illuminate our minds and hearts concerning the people we serve. Otherwise, we could make a grave error and, while offering the meat of the word, choke spiritual babes.

The mid to late 1900s brought about a cultural group known as "hippies." They were characterized by tie-dye tee shirts, long hair, free spirits, and peace signs (to mention a few). It was not uncommon for hippies to adorn themselves with stylish wire-rimmed sunglasses. The lens colors would vary. Some would be rose colored, some yellow, some green, and so forth. Whatever color glasses were worn would determine what color the world appeared to the viewer. Regardless of the truth, if you had on rose colored glasses, everything would look rosy.[19]

The point is that too often we wear *spiritually colored glasses* that may or may not be the true representation of what is around us. It is the Holy Spirit's job to filter what we are seeing so that we perceive what God would have us to see. We cannot and must not take things at face value. Otherwise, we will make a fatal *spiritual leadership mistake*. What is that mistake?

If not careful, we will find ourselves preaching on the symptoms rather than the real issues. Without God's guidance, we will find

---

18   The words, *"evaluated spiritually"* are rendered *"spiritually discerned"* in some translations, specifically KJV and NIV.

19   A technical term is used to denote this concept: "Operative Grid." An "operative grid" is that filter through which we see and understand life.

ourselves reacting to what we think we see or feel rather than what is genuinely real.

During my college years, I worked at a local grocery store where I kept the frozen food section well stocked. I had some fascinating experiences and met many great salesmen. On one occasion something happened that I will never forget.

The Kraft Food distributor observed a woman who was not particularly happy with me. Finally, I reacted and told her what I thought. Technically, what I said to her was correct, and no doubt she had it coming. She was rude not only to me, but to everyone in the store that day. Being the gentleman that he was, the distributor took me aside and said something that has stayed with me since 1976:

> "Mike, have you ever thought that the customer may have just come from the doctor and found out that she has terminal cancer? Have you ever considered that she may have just lost her father in an accident? Have you ever wondered if her husband may have just abused her? You never know where people are coming from, so be careful how you react."

This distributor of a major food company taught me an important lesson that day. I was interpreting the situation from my limited viewpoint instead of what might actually be happening. *But do you know what really hurt?* I was a ministerial student, but it took a salesman to teach me several truths:

o   Preachers do not have all the answers.
o   God uses laymen to help preachers understand life.
o   How I respond to others may be a test in my willingness to allow God to open my eyes to the culture around me.

This issue of cultural discernment may not always be easy to digest. Sometimes we must simply preach from our hearts and trust God to use our words to reach out to people wherever they are in life. God will not always give us a full, detailed analysis and understanding of our audience. This, however, does not diminish the importance of our performing due diligence in trying to understand the peoples' circumstances.

Hebrews 13:1-2 says, "Let brotherly love continue. Don't neglect to show hospitality, for by doing this some have welcomed angels (God's messengers) without knowing it." In other words, attempt to understand the situation, respond in love, meet needs, and realize that God is at work in all things.

Conclusion

A good preacher understands the culture, understands the Bible, and builds a sermonic bridge for people to walk *spiritually* from where they are to where they ought to be...and that is the Jesus model!

"Behold, I send you forth as sheep in the midst of wolves:
be ye therefore wise as serpents,
and harmless as doves"
(Matthew 10:16, KJV).

CHAPTER 7

CONTEXT

The Beginning Point

Many modern preachers are touting various philosophies and spiritual positions. A number of these issues are being proclaimed behind what has been classically known in evangelical churches as the "sacred desk."[20] The resources used as foundations for sermonizing are vast. However, just as God called preachers of the gospel, the only valid and reliable source provided by our Lord is the Bible. It is there that we must find the bedrock of those messages. Congregations gather expecting to hear a spiritual message from God. Holy Scripture must be the beginning point.

There are three issues to be clarified as we approach the Bible. Our goal is to understand, communicate, and apply scriptural truth. While this synopsis is in many ways over simplistic, its presentation is designed to be seen as a snapshot of the foundation for accurate biblical approach.

---

20   Old-time name for the pulpit.

> "Then He opened their minds to
> understand the Scriptures" (Luke 24:45).

Approach the Bible

Issues to be clarified as we approach the Bible:
- o   Assimilation
- o   Authorship
- o   Authority

Assimilation

The Bible consists of thirty-nine Old Testament and twenty-seven New Testament books. The sixty-six books were acknowledged early in history by Athanasius[21] in 367 A.D. The Old Testament was most likely intact prior to the time of Jesus. The New Testament went through various adjustments throughout the Second and Third Centuries. Eventually, after much prayerful evaluation and many spirited discussions, the formulation of what is known as the New Testament was finalized. The "canon" of sixty-six books was agreed upon and established. It has stood the test of time for the past 1,600 years.

Authorship

Every serious Bible scholar must wrestle with the concept of "AUTHORSHIP" and "authorship." Obviously, God is the AUTHOR. That is, He is the genesis, the beginning point, of all that is in the Bible. None of the Bible's substance was left to human intervention.

The author issue is one critically and often debated by scholars. At the end of the day one must ask, "How much of human element is in the Bible?" No doubt, God selected various personalities and styles to

---

21   Athanasius was the 20th bishop of Alexandria. He is known in some theological circles as the "Father of Orthodoxy."

communicate His Word. Liberal expositors would heighten the input of human elements. Their conclusion would be that the Bible "contains the word of God." More conservative scholars would hold to totally Divine authorship which would deny that the Bible *contains* the word of God, but rather that it *is* the word of God.

Authority

There have been numerous questions regarding the authority of the Bible. Ultimately, one must determine if God is, indeed, the AUTHOR. If the answer is yes, then the result must be perfect (because God is perfect). If the Bible is perfect, then it must stand as the final authority for the faith and practice of every devoted follower of Jesus Christ. Just as the United States Supreme Court is the final word on the rule of law in our land, so also is the Bible the final Supreme Authority on all matters of life.

In response to biblical authority, someone commented, "God said it; I believe it; and that settles it." However, the truth is: If God said it, that settles it…whether anyone believes it or not!

One's conviction and position on biblical authority will directly impact the ability to proclaim a message from God's Word. Weak confidence in scriptural truth will yield weak pulpit skills. A firm conviction regarding the truth of God's Word will enhance a biblical preacher's ability to stand before congregations and say, "Thus saith the Lord."

Infallible? Inerrant?

Two controversial words have been used to describe the Bible: INFALLIBLE and INERRANT. While these words polarized many sincere Bible scholars, one summed it up with a basic, yet profound thought.

All political nuances aside, this preacher said, "I will use 'inerrant,' 'infallible,' or any other positive adjective humans can conjure in regards to the Bible." Either the Bible is truth or it is not truth. Every preacher must decide where he stands, realizing that his decision will impact the spiritual journey and eternal destination of countless people.

On a personal note, I gave considerable thought to some who have questioned my firm stance on the authority of God's Word. I began to rest easy as God brought a thought to my spirit. When I die and go to heaven, I do not believe God will ever say to me, "Mike, you believed too much about My Word. You took it too literally and too seriously." I do believe, however, the possibility is real that when my life is judged that God could say, "Mike, why didn't you believe Me? It was right there in My Word!" If I find myself in error, I choose to err on the side of believing too much rather than too little.

Stages of Biblical Sermonic Development

As the preacher rises to open God's Word and proclaim its truth to listeners, four things must happen. Without disregarding the leadership of the Holy Spirit in the speaker and listeners, the preacher needs to walk through the following process:

- **Explain the text** (Chapter 7)
- Illustrate the text (Chapter 8)
- Apply the text (Chapter 9)
- Call for a response to the message (Chapter 9)

Explanation

The Text

The remaining portion of this chapter will deal with how to arrive at the intended content of the text. In order to adequately explain something, an understanding and valid contextual awareness is necessary. We must allow the text to speak for itself. In order to do so, we must know what is in it.

Often, preachers will use a passage to defend some personal agenda or issue that is totally foreign to what the Bible is attempting to address. This is known as "proof texting." One takes a subject and attempts to find some scriptural foundation for holding a certain position. The merits of the position may or may not be well-founded; however, it is always best to begin with what the Bible says and allow it to address what it will. The preacher's job is "exegesis" rather than to "eisegesis."[22] The following developmental roadmap for biblical study is a safe path towards solid biblical preaching.

- Read the text.
- Approach the text.
- Ask God for an immediate devotional thought.
- Write a one-sentence purpose statement of the text.
- Research the historical setting for the text.
- Study key words in the text.
- Research what others have to say about the text.
- Develop a summary on God's desired response to the text.

Read the text
Arriving at the text - How can we read the text when we do not know where to begin?

---

22   Interestingly, Wikipedia has one of the more clear and forthright definitions and explanations of this word. It offers a concise contrast to the appropriate method of scriptural study. It asserts, *Eisegesis* (from <u>Greek</u> εἰς 'into' and ending from *exegesis* from ἐξηγεῖσθαι 'to lead out') is the process of misinterpreting a text in such a way that it introduces one's own ideas, reading into the text. This is best understood when contrasted with *exegesis*. While *exegesis* draws out the meaning from the text, *eisegesis* occurs when a reader reads his/her interpretation into the text."

In 37 years of ministry, this has been one of my most difficult challenges. If a preacher has the responsibility of addressing the same group of people week after week, this can be a monumental hurdle. My process embraces some significant questions. Although the list is not exhaustive, it does address some of the ways the leading of God's Spirit may be sought:

- o   What cultural issues (Chapter 6) are impacting the everyday lives of our people?
- o   What everyday hurdles seem to impede the people?
- o   What issues or emphases in the church need to be scripturally clarified?
- o   What social issues are demanding people to make life decisions?
- o   What are the real (or perceived) needs of people?
- o   What temptations are people encountering?
- o   Where are people hurting?
- o   What spiritual blockades need to be overcome?

In more recent times, I am consciously asking, "If Jesus were bringing the message, what would He say?" (This is very likely the most critical question of all!)

Something that is most profitable to those who speak to the same congregation on a regular basis is to preach expository messages through the books of the Bible. This can help take the pressure off of "What comes next?" thought process. It also provides some continuity in taking people deeper in their walk with God.

The decision concerning which book to use may be arrived at in the same way one would arrive at a particular message (using the aforementioned questions). Different biblical books will offer different biblical solutions. For instance, if there are practical issues, the book of *James* is a great resource. If there are problems in the church, the books of *Corinthians* offer insight. The Gospels offer perspectives on the life and interactions of Jesus while bodily on earth. There is no better church growth book than *The Acts of the Apostles* (which is better entitled *The Acts of the Holy Spirit*). In other words, a selection should be made with regards to the needs of listeners.

Approach the text

Throughout my tenure as pastor, I have always attempted to use the same Bible to read, study, and carry to the pulpit. (Recently I have begun to also use a Bible on an electronic tablet in the pulpit.) That way I can make notations that are always available. In sermon preparation, I try to use the same Bible that I use in the pulpit. In my library, there are over 100 different Bibles. I have never counted the number of translations, but there are many. One must determine the translation that provides the most spiritual confidence and make it the primary resource. Other translations may be used to offer differing slants and insights. I do, however, recommend that a preacher use one main Bible a majority of the time.[23]

Ask God for a devotional thought

"How happy is the man who does not
follow the advice of the wicked,
or take the path of sinners, or join a group of mockers!
Instead, his delight is in the LORD's instruction,
and he meditates on it day and night.
He is like a tree planted beside streams of water
that bears its fruit in season and whose leaf does not wither.
Whatever he does prospers"
(Psalms 1:1-3).

Good preaching comes from the devotional overflow of Bible reading and the spiritual journey of God's servants. A God-called leader must

---

23   I do have particular Bibles that I use for weddings, funerals, and other special occasions that differ from the main pulpit Bible that is used from week to week.

learn before he can *lead*. More times than not, the devotional thought impressed on the heart of a preacher through a particular text is the spiritual fare God has in store when His people come to feast at the banquet table. As one scholar said, "preachers ought to preach out of the overflow." That overflow comes from biblical meditation. We ought to read the text over and over again.

> ## A God-called leader must learn before he can lead!

We cannot separate who we are from what God is trying to say. As discussed in Chapter One (CALLING), you were set apart for a defined purpose. God chose you...knowing your heart, personality, passions, and spirit. If the Bible does not come alive in your life as the message is being developed, then it most likely will not be very effective. However, do not be disheartened if the devotional thought is not immediate. Sometimes it takes pouring over a text for hours before that "eureka moment"[24] hits. Sometimes the listeners will even have a different "eureka moment" than the preacher. The Holy Spirit knows the need of each individual and often takes what we say and applies it to the particular needs of the congregation.

Write a purpose statement of the text

After having selected and devotionally read a text, one should write a brief purpose statement of what is being said. For example, John 3:16 says:

---

24 "Eureka moment" is a personal concept that I use to define that point in time when, after grappling with a text, it seems to reach out and grab me. This can be a highly charged spiritual moment or it may be a subtle sigh of awe and majesty. Regardless, there needs to be a point in the process where God's Spirit reaches out and grabs the heart of the preacher. That is when the "good stuff" comes!

"For God loved the world in this way:
He gave His One and Only Son,
so that everyone who believes in Him will not perish
but have eternal life."

The purpose of John 3:16 is to communicate God's redemptive plan which reclaims sinful humans and restores their relationship with Him forever.

Everything that is included in the sermon should support the overall purpose of what God is saying. While there may be many other good ideas that could be communicated, the preacher should always keep in mind the text's purpose. This will enhance the communication process and will restrict temptations to "chase rabbits"[25]

Research the historical setting for the text

"Then beginning with Moses and all the Prophets, He interpreted for them the things concerning Himself in all the Scriptures" (Luke 24:27).

Where do I find it?

One need not delve into deep theological volumes in order to understand the historical settings for the Bible. Most commentaries will give an overview of background information. Another simple location would be Bible dictionaries. This author uses the *Holman Bible Dictionary* because of its commitment to biblical truth and its Baptist affiliation. While not always dependable, certainly the internet will provide opportunities to quickly get a grasp on various aspects regarding the historical setting of a particular era. Preachers need to account for the authors of such resources and understand their particular position and approaches to the Bible. Remember, just because it is in print does not make it so (unless it is in *this book*—and yes, humor is good for the soul).

---

25 "Chase rabbits" is the process of departing from the text.

Who wrote it?

The importance of *authorship* helps to understand the vantage point from which the text originates. For instance in Psalm 23 the author writes, "The LORD is my shepherd." That is a magnificent statement that stands on its own. However, as one realizes that the author is King David, who served as a shepherd boy, our understanding of the text becomes richer. The author intimately knew what he was talking about. It is rich with meaning and application. The pastoral motif and nuances within the entire Psalm may be examined for meaning and application. Whereas, if the author had a limited knowledge or no experience at all with sheep, there would be less depth and less spiritual insight.

To whom was it written?

The recipients are important because it allows the reader to know what issues were being addressed. *Why write something to people where there is little to be applied?* Understanding the nature of those who would be reading the words enhances understanding in how the text should be read and what applications might be made.

A classic example of this is the Corinthian communication found in Paul's letters. The reason we know so much about this church is because they had so many problems. Their issues become beneficial to modern readers, because we can identify with where they were and understand how God addressed their misgivings. As the Bible says, "there is nothing new under the sun" (Ecclesiastes 1:9). Identifying with the recipients helps us know how to respond to the truth presented in God's Word.

For what purpose was it written?

As has already been mentioned, the purpose for writing the text becomes the purpose for preaching the text. If we do not determine why something was written, it becomes very difficult to know how to respond. The Bible was never given just so we would have *information*. It is given so we might experience *transformation*. The purpose of a text allows us to know what area needs to be transformed.

> **The purpose for writing the text becomes the purpose for preaching the text.**

Study key words in the text

One does not have to be a Greek or Hebrew scholar to do word studies. There are numerous resources available by way of books and online helps that will assist even a novice in understanding biblical words. Perhaps the most famous resource is *Strong's Concordance*. There is a reason God used the languages He used in the Bible. The Hebrew language is very basic and the Greek language is very advanced. The precision with which something may be communicated and articulated in the New Testament is enhanced due to the Greek.

One obvious place where the language makes a huge difference is in Jesus' dialogue with Peter in John 21. The word Jesus used for "love" and the word Peter used for "love" are two different words. It makes all of the difference in the world in how this text can be approached and preached. While the English translation is correct in both cases, the Greek is more precise. The Greek communicates more than the English is able to capture.

Although one may not be a Greek scholar, it will strengthen the message if the pastor is able to explain what is actually being said beyond an obvious reading in the English. Remember, the information learned is only as good as the source. Trusted resources should be used. Those resources may be located by researching respected sources and finding out where they turn for information.

A final thought on this subject—just because a person may support an opposing view on some theological issue does not mean that his resource should not be studied. The reader simply needs to be aware of what a particular author believes (in order to guard against erroneous conclusions) and then proceed wisely.

Research what others have to say about the text

Biblical commentaries are probably the most common resources to assist preachers in developing messages. I heard a very astute and popular preacher say that there is so much information out there that one can become overwhelmed with too much information. He suggested that a preacher get four or five dependable commentaries and let them be the bedrock for sermonic development. This does not mean that other resources will not be used periodically, but it does prevent one from becoming bogged down in research.

There is a very good reason that I have positioned the discussion on the use of commentaries at this point in our dialogue about sermon preparation. Commentaries should *not* be the first place a preacher goes. Why? Because this will short circuit allowing the Holy Spirit to guide and teach you before you hear what He has taught others. One will be surprised how many times the Holy Spirit has already led you to the same thoughts that others have gleaned—and that is a Divine confirmation that you are on the right course.

Develop a summary of God's desired response

Now that you have done all of this work, you are ready to preach, right? NO!

There is still considerable work to do. Once there has been a thorough Bible study, the material needs to be compiled and digested. As you contemplate the mounds of notes and thoughts, begin a list of the most important concepts that surface. Just as the *cream rises to the top* when it sits for a while, so the *cream* of God's Word rises to the top after being given time to settle. The *cream* will become the outline for the preacher's message.

Conclusion

Solid biblical hermeneutics[26] means that we attempt to get right at exactly what God desires to say. The Bible ends by saying: "I testify to everyone who hears the prophetic words of this book: If anyone adds to them, God will add to him the plagues that are written in this book. And if anyone takes away from the words of this prophetic book, God will take away his share of the tree of life and the holy city, written in this book" (Revelation 22:18-19).

This means we want to get it right. By taking the major truths and making them the major points, we ensure that we stay on target. Some use literary devices (such as alliteration) to make the points, and periodically that is perfectly fine. One never should allow the communication device, however, to become the focal point. We want people to hear the truth. The truth is God's Word, not our clever way of stating it.

"For the Word of God
is living and effective and
sharper than any two-edged sword,
penetrating as far as to divide soul, spirit, joints,
and marrow; it is a judge of the ideas and thoughts of the heart"
(Hebrews 4:12).

But even now, we are not finished. The next step is to develop the devices which will adequately communicate the biblical truth in a way that it will be properly received and understood.

---

26 *Webster's Online Dictionary* defines hermeneutics as "methodological principles of interpretation."

CHAPTER 8

COMMUNICATION

Bridging Biblical Truth to
Personal Understanding

Good communication requires the leadership of the Holy Spirit…as well as lots of hard work from the preacher!

The entirety of material prior to this chapter deals with getting an accurate handle on biblical truth. There are many excellent scholars who have done remarkable studies in areas related to theology and the Bible; however, often they have difficulty conveying what they know to others. Paul admonishes his young understudy, Timothy, to communicate to others what he has learned. Paul writes:

"And what you have heard from me in the presence of many witnesses, commit to faithful men who will be able to teach others also" (2 Timothy 2:2).

It is not enough for leaders to know what the Bible says. God's plan is that we be conduits, not containers. We must communicate to others what God has taught us so they can be and do all that God is calling them to be.

> **Three Components of An Effective Sermon**
> **Explanation** (Chapter 7)
> **Illustration** (Chapter 8)
> **Application** (Chapter 9)

The art of communication is difficult. It is often easier to learn something than it is to transfer it to others. It takes the Holy Spirit's leadership, discernment, study, and hard work. The bridge between what the Bible says and how it is to be applied is found in what is known as an ILLUSTRATION. Its importance is obvious. An illustration walks people from the truths in the Bible to where they can understand it and apply it in life.

The art of effective textual illustration is what separates fair sermons from great sermons. Great Bible scholarship and study does not automatically offer up a great message. Bridging biblical truth to congregational understanding requires unique and effective communication skills. Locating and applying appropriate illustrations can make a huge difference.

The dictionary definition of "illustration" is "to enlighten" or "to light up."[27] The English root comes from the Latin word meaning "to purify or make bright." Therefore, a good sermonic illustration takes the biblical text and highlights the intended meaning. This will enlighten the listener and give a clearer picture of what is actually being said.

---

27 *Webster's Online Dictionary.*

Biblical Illustrations

"And He did not speak to them without a parable. Privately, however, He would explain everything to His own disciples" (Mark 4:34).

Parables

Biblical confirmation that appropriate illustrations are acceptable comes from Jesus Himself. He was a master of motifs[28] and illustrations. Perhaps His favorite form of illustration was the parable. An unknown source has tagged the definition of a parable as "an earthly story with a heavenly meaning." Very simply, a parable is a story (genuine or designed) that sheds light on a heavenly concept. Generally, there is one central meaning in a parable. A story with multiple meanings is known as an allegory. While allegories are used in the Bible,[29] Jesus' favorite mode of storytelling was the parable.

Stories were used in such manner prior to the time of Jesus. One of the most famous Old Testament usages is when Nathan used a story to illustrate David's guilt (2 Samuel 12:1-4). Obviously the focal point of Nathan's story is the guilt of King David in his illicit relationship with Bathsheba and his mistreatment of her husband Uriah.

It was through parabolic devices that Jesus illustrated kingdom concepts. In fact, Jesus communicated kingdom truths through many different parables. Jesus himself appears indirectly in the story of the house divided against itself in Mark 3:23-27. "The parables are not

---

28 Someone has calculated over 100 motifs (designs) used to describe the various tasks assigned to God's people. These simply illustrate the purpose of what God's people ought to be about (i.e., *ambassadors, royal priesthood, and the body*).

29 Ezekiel 17 has a story with different meanings assigned to various parts of the story. Some famous historical allegorical works are *Pilgrim's Progress* and *Gulliver's Travels*.

merely clever stories but a proclamation of the gospel. The audience must respond and is invited by the story to make a decision about the kingdom and the King."[30]

The question arises concerning using various intricacies of a parable to illustrate various points. Generally, the answer is in the negative. Most of the time parables should be interpreted as having only one main major point. However, when Jesus goes into detail in His stories, as in the prodigal son (Luke 15), some feel that there are allegorical tendencies within the parable. In other words, there are numerous points that can be derived. *Why else would Jesus go into such detail?*

The purpose of this work is not to debate such matters of interpretation. Each preacher of the gospel must come to grips with how he deals with that question. The point of this section is to underscore the fact that Jesus used stories (real and imagined) to point out various characteristics of God's kingdom. In fact, the illustrations were often used to enlighten the critics. Jesus attempted to make it plain and simple.

Use common sense regarding illustrations
1. The illustration ought to illustrate the biblical material that has just been presented. Relevancy and a direct correlation to what God is saying is the bottom line. It ought to:
   o   Have a pertinent point to the aforementioned text.
   o   *Not* simply be an interesting story.
   o   *Not* be designed to aggrandize the presenter. (Remember, illustrations do not need to bring attention to the intelligence level of the preacher.)
   o   *Not* be inserted simply to add humor.
   o   *Not* be designed to inject some political or philosophical preference.

---

30 *Holman Bible Dictionary.*

2. The illustration ought to be as concise as possible. The longer it becomes, the more attention is brought to the illustration, removing the focus from the biblical text.
3. The illustration ought to be reliable and true unless otherwise noted.
4. The illustration ought not to be "trumped up" or "colored up" in order to make it more graphic. It is what it is, and it will be most effective when it is left that way.
5. Personal illustrations are acceptable with the following caveats:
   o Keep it minimal with regards to the preacher's family.
   o If family illustrations are used, all parties ought to give their approval.
   o Avoid personal aggrandizement or degradation.
6. Any use of appropriate humor ought to apply to the point of the biblical text.
   o There are places in the sermon where it is appropriate to insert a little humor to lighten the load of material that is being presented. However, to tell a joke just to be funny is not why we are in the pulpit. If folks wanted a comedy show, they would go to a theater.
   o Funny stories are excellent tools of communication. However, no preacher wants the listeners to leave worship remembering the funny story and missing the point of the sermon. Always drive the biblical truth home after telling the story.
   o Appropriate humor is a key. One needs to know the audience and culture as best as possible. What may be funny in Knoxville, Tennessee may not be so humorous in New York. Typically, humor and jokes do not work well cross-culturally. When using a translator in preaching, it is best to avoid jokes all together. American jokes seldom translate well in other languages.

7. Illustrations need to be used with discretion, avoiding any hint of insult because of:

Race ~ This is not just a black/white issue. There are many hues of color in the human race. All have equal value and must be treated with the ultimate love and respect that God offers.

Religious Preference ~ Belittling non-Christians or people from another denomination shows a lack of class, plain and simple. The truth is that there will be people in heaven who have differing theological views on earth. Illustratively insulting any group may hinder one's ability to communicate what God desires to say.

Gender ~ There is no room for a gender-neutral Bible. God is HE! Publishers who choose to develop politically correct material are being intellectually dishonest with the text.

Illustrations affecting people, however, ought not to shed a negative light on either gender. We are all just people. "Gender bashing" in an illustration will isolate that specific group in the congregation.

Political Views ~ Jesus is not a Republican or a Democrat. Illustrations must be easily received by people from all walks of life. This is not to say that preachers ought to stay away from issues in politics, but one must use care in communicating the biblical truth.

Idiosyncrasies of Communities Where Message Is Being Delivered ~ The issue of sensitivity regarding the community cannot be overstated. If people in the congregation are insulted, it is very difficult to gain a hearing of biblical truth. Cultures are different even within the confines of a city limits. A preacher should attempt to understand the hearts and minds of the audience when delivering illustrative material.

8. If an illustration is offered and told as if it were true, it ought to be so. If not, somewhere on either side of the illustration there are several ways to offer disclaimers. If one either knows it is not true or if one is unsure they may simply say:

   o Prior to illustration: "I cannot document what I am about to share, but…"

   o After illustration: "That did not really happen."

9. Do not cite material you have retrieved from outside sources as if it were your own. Plagiarism (stealing other people's material) is not an acceptable practice in the ministry. Someone said, "If you cite one source without giving credit, that's plagiarism. If you cite five sources, that's research." The point is that if we tell it as a first hand story, it needs to actually be a first-hand story. If we share something we have heard or read, we need to simply say: "I recently read…" or "I once heard…"

Integrity should not only be applied at the level of biblical study, it needs to be true throughout the entire message. My listing of generalities obviously is not exhaustive; however, every preacher ought to carefully and skillfully develop the art of offering illustrative material that will enhance the message, not detract from it.

> An illustration should enhance the message, not detract from it.

Locating Illustrations

Where *not* to find illustrations

Probably just as important as where to find illustrations is where <u>not</u> to find them. Preachers ought not to fall into the trap of telling stories that have characters where the identity of its subject is obvious. Constituents within the congregation may be deeply hurt or become disenfranchised.

Referencing local town gossip may cause some to feel the preacher is taking sides or meddling in areas where they are obviously misinformed. Stay away from community gossip. True or false, the preacher can get burned.

Confidential meetings in the pastor's study need to stay that way. Once a counseling session becomes public knowledge from the pulpit, the preacher has lost a trust that is nearly impossible to regain. Never assume that people will not know of whom you are speaking.[31]

Illustrative sources

One good source for textual illustrations is the Bible. There are many stories in the Bible that can be used to offer enlightenment on other texts. Do not be afraid to reference other passages in the Bible. Simply make sure they actually do offer enlightenment. Sometimes more questions can be raised than answers offered.

- o There are many reputable books that are designed to offer topical arrangements of illustrative material. Usually, when the editor is one of reputable character, these stories have been documented and substantiated.
- o There are numerous websites on the internet that offer illustrative material. Some are designed to pull up a particular passage and numerous applicable illustrations appear. Others, like most books, are topical in nature and have sermon enhancements listed by subject.

31　I have actually told stories that had nothing to do with counseling sessions, but because they were similar, some felt I had betrayed them. Even though I would never do that, it took a long time for me to convince them. Sometimes preachers do not stay long enough to overcome such issues. These just go with the territory and there is little, if anything, that can be done. When in doubt, find another illustration.

o Public issues are some of the most effective snapshots of where people are living. Everyday life identifies what is on the minds and hearts of most people. Life stories from the news can be very effective tools for clarifying God's Word.

o Various forms of media bring life stories into our lives each and every day. Preachers ought to stay abreast on current events.

o A preacher's personal experience has its positive and negative aspects relative to shedding light on God's Word.

The following should be remembered:

o The illustration shows the humanness and transparency of the preacher.

o The illustration in no way should make the speaker the hero. This is not a time for a personal ego boost.

o The passion with which one expresses a story is often much more emblazoned when it is told in the first person. When we experience something, we can share it with much more vim and vigor.

o Life offers some of the best illustrative material (i.e., children on the way to church). If you are telling a story involving someone you know, always gain permission. In today's world, it might not be a bad idea to get it in writing. That removes all doubt.

One area in which a preacher must exercise extreme caution is in regard to funeral stories. One of the more somber places where personal illustrations are used is during a memorial service of the deceased. The preacher ought to take great care in eulogies. My personal experience is that the eulogy ought to include no more than one or two stories involving a person's life. No matter how good a person may have been, there are always those who could probably state otherwise. The preacher loses credibility by simply not knowing all of the facts. There is no debate regarding dates and loved ones. However, to illustrate the "godliness" of an individual by how they lived life can be dangerous. I am not saying to totally refrain. I am saying to keep it at a minimum. Remember, you are there ultimately to communicate God's Word (comfort, conviction, conversion) to those who remain. Just be careful about saying too much. The Bible (Jesus) says, "No one is good but One—God" (Luke 18:19).

Appearance

I was once at a conference in a Baptist college where the preacher delivered a chapel sermon entitled: "Making Jesus Lord of Your Life." Upon leaving the chapel service, one of the students remarked, "I have a difficult time respecting that man." "Why?" I asked. The student remarked, "Because he obviously weighs over 350 pounds. If he wanted to preach on Jesus being Lord of his life, why did he not mention gluttony? It all seemed disingenuous to me."

His point was well made. We are not perfect. We may not be able to purchase an expensive suit of clothes, but we can attempt to honor our Lord with how we look. *If we were entering into the presence of an earthly king, what would we wear? Would we be groomed? Would our appearance be appropriate?*

The point of this section is not to advocate a coat and tie for every sermon. It is, however, to make the point that sometimes people will miss what we say if there is a violation of certain dress codes. There are places where blue jeans and open collared shirts are acceptable. There are also times when one needs to be in his very best. The "dress" needs to be to the level of where everyone in the room will feel comfortable. Anything less will be distracting.

Passion

Preach it as if you believe it. If there is any appearance of reservation of your belief in what you are saying, people will pick up on it. Even if you do not say it, folks are very intuitive. They will be able to discern your commitment to what you are saying. If you do not believe it, do not be hypocritical. Remember—the Bible is not on trial, but we are. Ask God to change your heart and give you a passion for what you are saying. It will make a difference.

Delivery/Inflection

The most important part of the message is the substance of what is being said. However, if nobody is listening, what good does it do? While the insomnia of some listeners may be cured, there is little impact from a sermon that is poorly delivered.

The Bible is full of commands. As those texts are referenced, it is totally appropriate to inject a commanding authority in the vocal delivery. Actually, to read a command in a passive, non-passionate manner is a misinterpretation of what the Bible is saying. If it says it strong, say it strong.

Jonathan Edwards is a perfect example that a monotone sermon can have dynamic results. However, that happened during a time when there was a great prayer movement amongst God's people. There was a hunger and an expectation (but remember...we are not Jonathan Edwards).

Monotone messages are often read from a manuscript. If you use a full manuscript, memorize it. Do not read it. Use your voice to illustrate the various points in the message. If there is textual tension, allow it to be heard and felt by the hearers. If there is reflection, become soft in tone. Allow what is being said to be heard in the vocal projection.

One of the most disturbing things about some preachers is that they choose to yell at congregations during the entire message. Nobody wants to be yelled at. However, there are some who do not believe you have preached unless you 'scorch them.'

Learn to project from the diaphragm (lower portion of the abdomen). A casual voice will often not be heard, even with the best electronic equipment. Project your voice, but not from the throat (as most old time preachers). This will ruin the ability to last for the long haul, and it is not very appealing to the ears. One great orator told me that he worked for years developing his voice. He was one of the best. We all could learn that lesson.

Mobility

Physical[32] ~ Sometimes walking from one side of the pulpit to the other augments what is being said. At other times, it is a distraction. The size of a room or the proximity of the stage area can determine how mobile the preacher can be. When away from the pulpit area for any length of time, it is a good idea to have Bible in hand. I keep my notes or outline in the Bible so that if I am away from the pulpit, I still have access to where I am in the message.

Eyesight ~ Looking at your audience eyeball to eyeball can be very intimidating. Some speech classes teach speakers to span the back wall (back and forth, left and right) in order to give the illusion that you are making eye contact with the audience. This should also be practiced in areas where lighting is bright and the preacher may not be able to see his audience.

A good practice is to be so focused on the message that the audience is not a distraction. I attempt to give the appearance that I am looking right at everyone in the room. I also always attempt to keep a genuine smile on my face so the people will see a pleasant delivery.

---

32 Nervous habits should be brought under control while in the pulpit. Unnecessary motions will only detract from what is being said. Examples would be constantly fiddling with buttons, glasses, etc.

Kinesiology

Kinesiology is simply the study of human movement. Animation may be both an enhancement and/or a distraction. Body language is a vital part of communication. For example, palms turned downward indicate distance. Palms upward indicate openness. Raising hands as a form of praise is certainly an appropriate biblical practice. Psalm 63:4 says, "So I will praise You as long as I live; at Your name, I will lift up my hands." This is a good place for the preacher to demonstrate the practice of raised hands in times of worship and praise. Raised hands are symbolic of surrender and honor.

Body movement needs to always match the message. We need to always be aware of our non-verbal language, facial expressions, and potentially distracting habits. Nothing detracts more than motions which have nothing to do with the subject matter. They actually take away from and can become a psychological block to effective communication.

Grammar

A general definition of "grammar" includes how words relate in some sort of systematic or acceptable fashion. Incorrect usage of words will quickly distract your listeners. Basic principles of grammatical communication ought to be observed by the preacher. Failure to do so may damage the effectiveness of the message.

During a revival service many years ago, I heard an excellent, fiery message by a very gifted evangelist. He was obviously not a very well-educated man, but his heart and passion for the gospel were obvious. He was also "right on" when it came to theological issues; however, during his message, he absolutely slaughtered the King's English. He was intelligent enough to know that he had misused some words. Without missing a beat he commented, "That may be bad grammar, but it is good theology." While making his point very effectively, I could not help thinking that God wants our best.

The importance of good word usage is, I think, a sign of how much we truly care about what we are saying. To know what is theologically correct is one thing. If we desire to maximize our impact, we need to take the time and energy to learn how to communicate it properly. While the preacher may not know the Greek and Hebrew languages, he does need to have a fairly good grasp of the English language.

In some cultures, various misuses are acceptable. While it may be socially acceptable, the preacher does not need to fall into that trap. If you learn it correctly and use it correctly, you can say it anywhere and it will not matter. How we say things may be just as important as what we are saying; otherwise, we may communicate an unintended message.

Conclusion

Connecting biblical truth to people is a difficult task. Developing the art of effective communication is a lifelong study and a work in progress. Through God's leadership and diligence, the appropriate tools will surface.

How you say something can be as important as WHAT you say. The ultimate goal is spiritual transformation in the lives of listeners. As we glorify God, this will happen!

"Don't let your mouth speak dishonestly,
and don't let your lips
talk deviously" (Proverbs 4:24).

CHAPTER 9

CURRENCY

Approaching the Truth

F or if I preach the gospel, I have no reason to boast, because an obligation is placed on me. And woe to me if I do not preach the gospel (1 Corinthians 9:16).

Two distinctive interpretive errors occur when approaching the truth found in the Bible. First, it is simply seen as a book about events that happened over two thousand years ago; therefore, it is out of date and has little to offer in the high tech society prevalent today. The second is the prophetic error which simply means that the Bible's impact is futuristic and has no demands on an individual in the present. Both errors will lead to a fatalistic approach to the Bible.

As the Word of God is studied, preached, and taught, there needs to be an emphasis on the issue of currency. This means that what is being stated has current implications and demands a current response. The Bible was never revealed to simply give information about God. It is dynamic in that there are personal applications to be used in everyday life. Someone once said that regardless of the issue, the Bible has a principle or precept that, if followed, will bring the best result. This does not mean that we will always understand immediately, but it does mean that one day the blinders will be removed and as it unfolds we shall be able to grasp how everything fits together.

1 Corinthians 13:12 says: "For now we see indistinctly, as in a mirror, but then face to face. Now I know in part, but then I will know fully, as I am fully known."

Paul is emphasizing that we will not always understand, but by faith, we must make current applications knowing that one day it will all be made clear.

**His work is not for our destruction—
but rather for our deliverance!**

Romans 8:28 offers encouragement and assurance: "We know that all things work together for the good of those who love God: those who are called according to His purpose."

As we live our lives and apply God's truths, we may be assured that He is at work. His work is not for our destruction, but rather for our deliverance.

Jeremiah 29:11 says, "For I know the plans I have for you" —[this is] the LORD's declaration—"plans for [your] welfare, not for disaster, to give you a future and a hope."

We must simply live in the confidence that as we place into action the principles taught in God's Word, He will lead us toward His desired end—and that "end" is always in our best interest. Even though we cannot see it now, God is constantly working through our situations and circumstances to be most beneficial in our personal lives and in His kingdom work.

Proverbs 3:5-6 offers God's desired response on our part:

"Trust in the LORD with all your heart, and do not rely on your own understanding; think about Him in all your ways, and He will guide you on the right paths."

> **Three Components of An Effective Sermon**
> Explanation (Chapter 7)
> Illustration (Chapter 8)
> **Application** (Chapter 9)

Application

This section will deal with the immediate application of what has been explained. It is the third and final component of an effective biblical sermon. After the material has been sifted and understood, the time has come to engraft it into the life of the listener. People must not only understand but apply the message.

For example, if a person contracted a terrible toxic disease, and the cure was formulated, made available, and even purchased by the patient, what good would it do if the medication remained in the packaging? Too often this is what happens to biblical truth. Sin has corrupted humans spiritually; God's Word reveals the cure. Just as the toxic patient can not be cured until the medicine is applied, neither can the Christian experience the intended spiritual remedy without "taking the medicine" of God's Word.[33]

---

33   Matthew 9:12 – "no need for."

The preacher cannot (and must not attempt to) force feed any congregation. However, he must offer clear and concise applications whereby the audience is fully aware of what is expected in response to the message. One of the great texts on the preacher's responsibility in relation to the listener is found in Ezekiel 33:7-11. The prophet writes:

> "As for you, son of man, I have made you a watchman for the house of Israel. When you hear a word from My mouth, give them a warning from Me. If I say to the wicked: 'Wicked one, you will surely die,' but you do not speak out to warn him about his way, that wicked person will die for his iniquity, yet I will hold you responsible for his blood. But if you warn a wicked person to turn from his way and he doesn't turn from it, he will die for his iniquity, but you will have saved your life.

> "Now as for you, son of man, say to the house of Israel: 'You have said this: Our transgressions and our sins are [heavy] on us, and we are wasting away because of them! How then can we survive?' Tell them: 'As I live'—the declaration of the LORD God—'I take no pleasure in the death of the wicked, but rather that the wicked person should turn from his way and live. Repent, repent of your evil ways! Why will you die, house of Israel?'"

The preacher is just the delivery boy!

The point of this section is clearly responsibility. It is the responsibility of the watchman to warn. It is the responsibility of the people to respond. The application is concise and clear. There is neither ambiguity nor vagueness. Very simply, the people in this passage are to "Repent, repent of your evil ways!" Failure to do so results in death!

The realization that a response will be expected at the end of the message should be maintained all throughout the sermon. Billy Graham began the invitation (indirectly) the moment he stood up to preach. In the back of his mind, he knew he would be calling lost people to Christ and saved people to make a fuller commitment. When we approach the message this way, we will preach with more direction and passion. The following pages offer some assistance in understanding and developing the relevancy, currency, and application portion of the message.

Conflict

The sooner we realize that we are in a spiritual battle, the sooner we can take steps to eliminate controllable roadblocks during the invitation. There are some things we just cannot control, but we can create an environment whereby Satan has less ground on which to take his stand. We *must* understand with whom we are dealing. This is *not only* a solemn time during the worship when we get quiet and people join the church. Oftentimes, some in the congregation are oblivious and begin making preparations to leave. However, we must realize this is a time when life and death decisions are being made. Our battle is with "the powers of this dark world."

> Ephesians 6:12 – "For our struggle is not against flesh and blood, but against the rulers, against the authorities, against the powers of this dark world and against the spiritual forces of evil in the heavenly realms." (NIV)

Satan does not want us to read our Bibles and pray. As we begin applying what the Bible says, Satan's diabolical interest peaks. He does not want us to connect biblical truth with our everyday lives. Spiritual warfare intensifies when people are at the point of application and decision. The conflict is not between the preacher and the prospect, but between Satan and God's Holy Spirit. We should not become too amazed or alarmed that opposition and distortion will often take place during this section of the message. Satan knows that with every biblical application there is one part of a person's life that he is losing. He will not take it sitting down. Conflict from him will ensue. *Why is this so?*

The half-brother of the Lord writes: "...don't you know that friendship with the world is hatred toward God? Anyone who chooses to be a friend of the world becomes an enemy of God" (James 4:4).

You are behind enemy lines!

When we begin speaking about life transformation issues, we are in enemy territory. Ultimately, every one of us must choose with which army we desire to enlist and serve. One thing is for sure, we will serve in one army or the other.

Jesus said, "Anyone who is not with Me is against Me, and anyone who does not gather with Me scatters" (Matthew 12:30).[34]

It is the job of the gospel preacher to bring people to a crossroad where a decision will be made. Remember, we can only lead people so far and then we must ask them to make a decision. Yogi Berra supposedly quipped to a reporter, "When you come to a fork in the road, take it." The truth is that every listener comes to a fork in the road. Jesus indicates that neglecting to make a decision to travel His road is an automatic decision to take the other road. A person cannot just stand still.

The Lord gave me an illustration that clearly defines this point. While changing planes in one of the world's largest airports, I had to

---

34   Matthew 12:30 – This is a statement of decision.

walk a rather lengthy distance to the next gate. This particular airport had moving sidewalks. Obviously, if you continue walking while on the moving sidewalk you can save valuable time. As I approached the end of the moving walkway, an elderly woman proceeded to get off, but then, she stopped. *The problem?* The people behind her could not stop. Thankfully, all of us were able to avoid falling on her. You can just imagine hustling passengers with briefcases and carry-on luggage suddenly coming to a halt...objects flying in a sundry of directions with that poor little woman at the bottom of the pile. In those situations, you have no choice. You must keep going.

When we get to the point of decision time in the sermon, there are no options. People must understand what Moses told the Israelites in Deuteronomy 30:11-18:

> "This command that I give you today is certainly not too difficult or beyond your reach... But the message is very near you, in your mouth and in your heart, so that you may follow it. See, today I have set before you life and prosperity, death and adversity. For I am commanding you today to love the LORD your God, to walk in His ways, and to keep His commands, statutes, and ordinances, so that you may live and multiply, and the LORD your God may bless you in the land you are entering to possess. But if your heart turns away and you do not listen and you are led astray to bow down to other gods and worship them, I tell you today that you will certainly perish and will not live long in the land you are entering to possess across the Jordan."

Joshua responded to a similar sentiment when he asserted:

"But if it doesn't please you to worship the LORD, *choose*[35] for
yourselves today the one you will worship…As for me and my
family, we will worship the LORD" (Joshua 24:15).

Often, the question arises at this point regarding predestination.
Do we decide? Does God choose? Certainly the Bible is clear when Jesus
says: "No one can come to Me unless the Father who sent Me draws
him…" (John 6:44). There are some who refuse to give an invitation,
claiming that the Father must and will handle that need in the lives
of those who are the chosen.

The purpose of this book is not to debate the merits of theological
issues where there are obvious question marks. Our purpose is to
simply offer a practical perspective that every gospel preacher-teacher
can use to effectively communicate a biblical message. The aim of
the message is a transformed life on the part of the listener. The Old
Testament writers offered people the opportunity for response. Jesus
and the New Testament writers proclaimed their messages in order for
people to respond. Nothing has changed. We, too, must give people the
opportunity to respond (understanding that Satan will do everything
possible to stop anyone from following God). The battle will intensify
at the point of making the message current: *The Invitation!*

The importance of making an immediate decision is found in
the words of the Lord Himself regarding the beginning of the human
experience (Genesis 6:3). He profoundly and clearly states: "Then the
LORD said, 'My Spirit will not contend with man forever…'" (NIV).
While it may be indiscernible on the human side, there can come a
point where a decision is no longer possible. The Old Testament speaks

---

35 "Choose" (*bāḥar*): (by implication) to make a selection. A primitive root. *Qal*:
Shem: Simple. Imperative mood. Compound.

of "hardened hearts."[36] The New Testament talks of God "delivering them over to degrading passions."[37]

How will this battle play out as the message is being delivered?

The following segment is not intended to be all-inclusive. It does, however, offer examples of what can happen. We cannot always stop distractions from happening, but we do not need to panic. The truth of 1 John 4:4 is especially applicable here: "You are from God, little children, and you have conquered them, because the One who is in you is greater than the one who is in the world." *So then, what will this look like?*

Distractions

Distractions in the life of the preacher

Satan is the author of confusion, and he will do everything in his power to distract the preacher during the point where the message is moving from explanation to application. These distractions come in one of two ways:

Internal Confusion ~ There is a loss of concentration and the preacher draws a mental blank. That is why it is beneficial to have a designed plan on exactly how to offer the invitation. If it is either written down (preferred) or memorized, you can always go back to the point where you left off. We will address this at a later point in this chapter.

External Movement ~ Something in the room gains the attention of the speaker. This may or may not be visible to the congregation, but it is very real to the preacher. Again, a designed plan helps. You can always go back to where you left off.

---

36 Exodus 9:12.

37 Romans 1:24, 26, 28.

Distractions in the congregation

This has many potential culprits. It can include stormy weather, electrical power failure, sound system glitches, a person in the congregation who has a distracting habit or cough, rowdy children or parents, etc. Satan uses many "innocent" situations to remove what God wants to do in the hearts and lives of people who have heard the Word of God.

On one occasion I was wrapping up the message and preparing to give the invitation. It was in a very small church that had no nursery. Suddenly I heard a noise and spotted a little boy on his knees moving towards the altar. He was pushing a toy tractor trailer and making the appropriate noise as if he were trucking down the interstate. I handled the situation poorly. Instead of acknowledging the humor, I called attention to the child (therefore the parents also) and said something to the effect that this was not appropriate in church.

Alternatives? Acknowledge the humor and remind people that regardless of what is distracting them, God wants them to follow Him. Or use the boy coming forward as a providential way to invite others to follow and make a decision for Christ.

Distractions in the life of the listener

The range of distractions varies greatly and might be psychological, emotional, practical, and the list goes on *ad infinitum*. Preachers need to understand that everyone has issues, and people within the same congregation will be coming with different concerns in all walks of life. As aforementioned, the most tense portion of the service is where God wants to address those issues…and Satan wants to stop Him!

When a huge wave hits you in the sea of life, you cannot quit rowing. You must keep going. The destination is worth it! The only way Satan can be victorious in our lives is if we become doubtful and stop. We must not allow temporal distractions to prevent us from proclaiming truth that can alter someone's eternal destiny. Do not hesitate; stay on course!

Calling for a Response

What is the preacher's responsibility in offering people the opportunity to respond to the message from God's Word? This is why we do what we do. We are not engaged by God to simply offer historical information. We are to present information that will lead to life transformation in the lives of the listeners. Like the "watchman" on the wall, we are responsible to call for a response.

What are some practical things that may be done at the time of the invitation that will maximize the invitation experience for the listener? Please understand that these suggestions are not in any way going to minimize the importance of the Holy Spirit's impact. We all understand that regardless of what we do, only the Holy Spirit can convert a lost soul or lead a follower of Christ into a deeper and richer experience with our Lord. However, this does not take away from our responsibility to create an atmosphere where one may sincerely consider the question that lies before them. There are several actions the preacher can take to position listeners for this time. Remember that only God's Spirit can lead people. If the listener chooses "no," that response will be honored by God. Also remember, no decision is a negative decision.

Some helps to consider:
1. *Begin the message with the understanding that there will be a time of decision at the end.*

Always keep the destination in mind. You are going to ask listeners to respond to what God has said and confirm in their personal lives the Lordship of Jesus Christ. This is true for "lost" and "saved" alike. Always be aware that you are delivering more than just interesting information about God. You are confronting people with the prospect of them making current what God is saying in His Word. The way they will do that is with a conscious decision that not only confirms what is taught but applies what has been taught.

Keep the destination in mind!

2. *Expect people to respond in the affirmative.*

If you enter a message thinking that nothing is going to happen, it probably will not. This is not the "power of positive thinking," but it is the power of bold application. In other words, if you expect people to say "yes" to biblical truth, you will preach with more boldness and confidence. In the end, it is not a confidence in oneself, but rather a confidence that God is going to do something. If you do not believe that, then why bother!!! When you open His Word, expect God to do great things. *Is there biblical confirmation for expectation?* Yes! God says:

> "For just as rain and snow fall from heaven, and do not return there without saturating the earth, and making it germinate and sprout, and providing seed to sow and food to eat, so *My word that comes from My mouth will not return to Me empty, but it will accomplish what I please,* and will prosper in what I send it [to do]." You will indeed go out with joy and be peacefully guided; the mountains and the hills will break into singing before you, and all the trees of the field will clap [their] hands" (Isaiah 55:10-12).

Expect people to respond!

3. *Do not be intimidated when it comes to asking people to make a decision.*

God has not given us a spirit of timidity or a wimpy way of expression and conviction. 2 Timothy 1:6-7 declares, "Therefore…keep ablaze the gift of God that is in you… For God has not given us a spirit of fearfulness, but one of power, love, and sound judgment."

There is a similarity in presenting the gospel to sales in the business world. Sales managers will affirm that it is not difficult to get their sales team to offer and explain the products; however, when it comes to asking for the sale, that is another matter. Many freeze at this point. Some even become embarrassed or apologetic. Obviously, they do not last very long.

A young student knocked on our door. With a colorful picture of a lovely flower garden in his hand, I quickly realized that his school was selling flower seed as a fundraising project. Our front porch introduction ran something like this:

"Hello, my name is Johnny (many ministerial stories have Johnny as the main character). I go to "Community School", and we are selling seeds to raise money for our upcoming field trip. They are beautiful flowers that will make your yard even more beautiful than it already is (Good Salesmanship!). *You don't want to buy some, do ya?"*

He was almost apologetic in asking for the sale. Unfortunately, many preachers fit into the same category. Due to a lack of expectation and confidence, we are often reticent in asking people to make a decision.

- o Solution: We should take comfort in the fact that Jesus did not stammer when it came to inviting people to respond.
- o Comfort: The best way to place a listener at ease is to be at ease.

One must be comfortable with the invitation. Comfort for the Great Commission Christian comes when one realizes that God desires each of us to invite people to Jesus. God certainly is not hesitant to challenge the listeners.

Through the prophet Isaiah He says: "<u>Come</u>, *all you who are thirsty, come to the waters; and you who have no money, come, buy and eat! Come, buy wine and milk without money and without cost*" (Isaiah 55:1, NIV).

Jesus, himself, was constantly referencing the concept of decisively following Him. He establishes the criteria for the rich young ruler.[38] He offers practical decisions for His disciples.[39] Perhaps the most pointed invitation given is found in Matthew 11:28 where He says: "<u>Come</u> *to me, all you who are weary and burdened, and I will give you rest*" (NIV).

> **God has not given us a spirit of fearfulness, but one of power, love, and sound judgment!**

Our comfort level in giving an invitation will put the congregation more at ease and create an atmosphere where it is easier to respond. People will pick up on any hesitancy on our part. That could cause them to be hesitant in responding. Be assured that Jesus was not hesitant. He called us to be bold as well…so…go for it, knowing that God is responsible for the results. We are not a success because people respond; we are successful when we are obedient!

4. *We must be clear in what we are asking people to do.*

For the first time in the history of America, we have a generation of adults who have never been to church. They do not know the songs, and many have never heard an organ outside the funeral home. They

---

38   Matthew 19:21.

39   Luke 9:23.

are unaware of anything about the Bible, and their concept of church is only what they have seen on television. For the most part, media outlets and entertainment venues have not presented a very flattering picture of the church; therefore, it is vital that we communicate with clarity exactly what we are asking people to do.

I have had the privilege of working in leadership roles with several evangelistic organizations (including Billy Graham's). As I listened to world renowned men give invitations, I noticed they gave explicit instructions. The flow would go somewhat like this:

> In about two minutes, I am going to lead you in a prayer. If you would like to receive forgiveness of your sins by trusting in Jesus as your personal Savior and Lord, I will ask you to join me as I pray.
>
> I will also include a prayer for those who have already accepted Christ and need to make a further commitment in some specific area of life.
>
> Then I am going to ask all who are making decisions to leave their seats and come forward. We will have people who want to pray with you and give you some literature. You will only be here a few short minutes.
>
> If you came with others, they will be able to meet you when we are through. Would each and every one of you bow your heads and close your eyes? If you would like to...repeat the following prayer...

Obviously, this is not an exhaustive list, but it demonstrates some components in giving a good invitation. People today do not want to be surprised or embarrassed. We need to let them know that they will not be expected to do anything that we have not informed them of beforehand. This will enhance the invitation experience.

Clarity on the part of those making a salvation decision is of utmost importance. Again, most people have no idea what it takes to become a follower of Jesus Christ and to go to heaven. We must plainly articulate that we are asking them to turn from sin, trust in Christ, and identify with His people. Jesus did not mince any words.

Very pointedly He laid it out, as uncomfortable as it may have been to some. Look at some prime examples of Jesus communicating how to make the gospel current in the lives of His listeners:

> *Matthew 16:24* – "Then Jesus said to his disciples, 'If anyone would come after me, he must deny himself and take up his cross and follow me.'" (NIV)

> *Luke 9:23* – "Then he said to them all: 'If anyone would come after me, he must deny himself and take up his cross daily and follow me.'" (NIV)

> *Mark 10:21* – "Jesus looked at him and loved him. 'One thing you lack,' he said. 'Go, sell everything you have and give to the poor, and you will have treasure in heaven. Then come, follow me.'" (NIV)

**Plainly articulate:
Turn from sin...
Trust in Christ...
Identify with His people!**

5. *As the preacher begins the time of invitation, there should be a notable shift in the presentation.*

Using phrases such as, "In a moment I am going to ask you to do something..." is a terrific way for the congregation to become emotionally involved in what is about to happen. Unfortunately, this is also the time when some will grab their coats or gather their belongings. Others simply go ahead and slip out. You have just informed them that the message is coming to a conclusion.

What can be done to keep the focus? The following techniques have proven helpful:

- Simply use a transitional statement: "We are about to enter the most important time of the service." This accentuates the importance of what is about to happen.
- Tell people why it is important. "Peoples' lives are hanging in the balance. The future of marriages is being decided this morning. The eternal destiny of someone is on the line."
- Let people know they can be a distraction to what God desires to do. "If you are not dealing with the issue of making some kind of decision, others around you are. Please pray for them as Satan attempts to keep them from doing what they are about to do."

At one point in the history of our church, people would actually leave as they were asked to bow their heads. I simply laid out the following instructions for the invitation:

"The only appropriate actions of anyone in this room are to

...sing the invitation hymn,

...pray for those who are contemplating decisions,

...or come forward to pray. Pray with one of our staff, pray at the altar, or inform one of our counselors of the decision you desire to make. Any other movement is inappropriate and may result in someone being distracted from doing what God has called them to do."

As this was done in all candor and love, the problem of people leaving during the invitation diminished.

While I have covered many practical helps for an effective invitation, it is important to note that not all of these are appropriate in every service. Use only the ones that are applicable for the moment.

The point is to create the best environment possible for people to make life-impacting decisions. The preacher laying out too many parameters for the invitation can become a distraction as well.

6. *The invitation needs to be clear and concise.*

Jesus demonstrated the most concise invitation ever recorded. When Peter wanted to get out of the boat and meet Him on the water, Jesus simply said, "Come!"[40]

The more words used means the more opportunity for confusion. This is no time for a major theological discussion or the time to relive and repreach the sermon. There is a great sentence that can transition the moment into a very effective sequence leading up to commitment:

> "Understanding what we have shared, would you like to receive this forgiveness by trusting in Christ as your personal Savior and Lord?"

This is clear and concise. Allow the people a moment to reflect and respond. Silence, here, is not a bad thing. A few seconds will allow them to process.

7. *Develop a prayer that can be used during every invitation.*

Every preacher needs to have such a prayer so there will be a natural flow. The prayer is such that people may recite it as it is being prayed. It needs to involve repentance and faith. The prayer I developed in 1977 and have used countless times inviting people to come to Christ goes like this:

Lord Jesus, I am a sinner,
I believe you died on a cross for me and shed your blood.
Right now, I turn from my sin. I give you my heart.

---

40   Matthew 14:29.

Come into my heart, Lord Jesus.
Thank you for saving me.
In your name, I pray.
Amen!

8. *Ask for a public response.*

Although a public response is unpopular in many circles, the Bible indicates there is merit to a public profession. The New Testament model has private confession followed by public profession in baptism. The mode of how people are introduced publically in their newfound faith may vary, but it needs to be done. Jesus said, "...everyone who will acknowledge Me before men, I will also acknowledge him before My Father in heaven" (Matthew 10:32).

9. *Lead people to do what is right.*

In the old days, the old time preachers called the invitation "drawing the net." This would be the time where "fishers of men"[41] could see the catch. Manipulation is never a good thing, but a preacher ought to lead people to do what is right. There are many techniques for "getting people down the aisle," and some are over the top. One way that appears to be acceptable is by having those who have made decisions raise their hands while heads are still bowed and eyes are still closed. The preacher is the only one looking (yeah...right). Anyhow, closing the invitation time can effectively be done in the following manner:

"Now I am going to ask you to open your eyes and look up here. Some of you made decisions that are very personal and important. You may be asking, 'What do I do now?' I am going to ask those of you who raised your hands for any reason to come forward as we begin singing. Come and tell one of our counselors (or "me" if you are the only one) about

41   Matthew 4:19 "Follow me, and I will make you fishers of men" (KJV).

the decision you just made. This would please God, and I know you want to bring honor to Him. Are you ready? If so, begin walking now as we begin singing…."

Conclusion

In no way does this material pretend to have all of the answers. Some of these approaches I use may not work for you. In the end, each individual servant of God must allow His Spirit to lead. As you are faithful and God is at work, precious lives will be touched for the kingdom. Think about it—you are selected and called to be a part. Now that is the wonder and grace of GOD!

> "Finally brothers, whatever is true, whatever is honorable, whatever is just, whatever is pure, whatever is lovely, whatever is commendable—if there is any moral excellence and if there is any praise—dwell on these things" (Philippians 4:8).

CPSIA information can be obtained at www.ICGtesting.com
Printed in the USA
LVOW120144060613

337156LV00001B/2/P